The SECOND KIDS' WORLD ALMANAC

OF RECORDS AND FACTS

OTHER BOOKS BY MARGO MCLOONE-BASTA AND ALICE SIEGEL

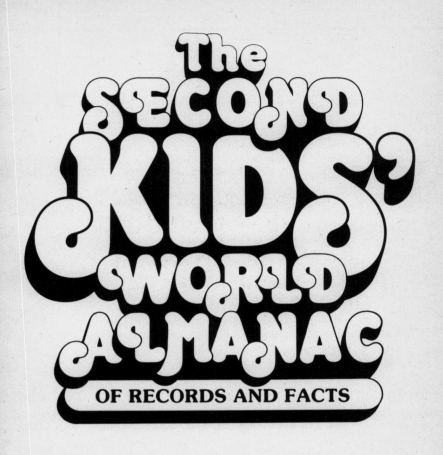

The SECOND KIDS' WORLD ALMANAC

OF RECORDS AND FACTS

**MARGO MCLOONE-BASTA AND ALICE SIEGEL
AND THE EDITORS OF THE WORLD ALMANAC**

Illustrated by John Lane

WORLD ALMANAC
AN IMPRINT OF PHAROS BOOKS • A SCRIPPS HOWARD COMPANY
NEW YORK

Book Design: Helene Berinsky
Illustrations: John Lane

First published in 1987.

Distributed in the United States by Ballantine Books, a division of
Random House, Inc., and in Canada by Random House of Canada, Ltd.

Library of Congress Cataloging-in-Publication Data:

McLoone-Basta, Margo.
The Second Kids' World Almanac of Records and Facts.

Includes index.
Summary: A reference book containing information
grouped in such categories as animals, body and health,
computers and robots, language, and religion.
1. Almanacs, Children's   [1. Almanacs]   I. Siegel,
Alice.   II. World almanac and book of facts.   III. Title.
AY81.J8M373   1987   031'.02   87-50101

Pharos Books ISBN 0-88687-317-7
Ballantine Books ISBN 0-345-34883-4

Printed in the United States of America

World Almanac
An Imprint of Pharos Books
A Scripps Howard Company
200 Park Avenue
New York, NY 10166

10 9 8 7 6 5 4 3 2 1

Pharos Books are available at special discounts on bulk purchases for sales promotions,
premiums fundraising or educational use. For details, contact the Special Sales
Department, Pharos Books, 200 Park Avenue, New York, NY 10166

For my family, George, Andrew, Howard and James.
—A.S.

For Douglas, Catherine and Elizabeth.
—M.M.B.

Contents

ACKNOWLEDGEMENTS

We greatly appreciate the enthusiasm of the kids, parents, teachers, librarians and fact lovers who have made this second volume of *The Kids' World Almanac* possible. There are many individuals to thank—all those people who have helped to find the answers to the questions kids ask. Our special thanks to Vicky Beal, Miriam Chaikin, Mary Chapman, Carol De Matteo, Debby Felder, June Foley, Ed Freidman, Mark Hoffman, Paul Hunter, Howard Land, Chris Merchant, Tom McGuire, Annie McLoone and Tom Moncrief of McLooney Tunes, Trish O'Connor, Rosemarie Semioli, Judy Sondheim, Michael Weinstein, M.D., Harmony Torres, Nutritionist, Lenox Hill Hospital, Mr. Koontz, Curator, The Bronx Zoo, and the wonderful librarians of the Greenwich, Connecticut, New York City, Scarsdale, and Woodstock, New York libraries.

The SECOND KIDS' WORLD ALMANAC

OF RECORDS AND FACTS

Animals the World Over

Are bats really blind? What's the difference between a dolphin and a porpoise? What is the daily menu of gorillas in the zoo? You'll find the answers to these and other questions about animals in this chapter. You will also be introduced to animal champions, history-making animals, mascots, and more. For animal lovers and the curious of mind, here is the world of animals.

Mistaken Notions About Animals

BATS ARE NOT BLIND

Most people think bats are blind, perhaps because many fly at night. All bats, whether they fly during the night or day, have excellent eyesight. How do night-flying bats find their way in the dark? They send out high-pitched cries which echo off objects. The sooner the echo returns to the bat, the closer the object is to the bat. In this way, the bat knows how to avoid crashing into things.

BEARS DO NOT KILL WITH A HUG
Bears kill their victims with a powerful swipe of their front paws. They do not give their enemies a "bear hug." Their arms are extremely strong and can strike lethal blows.

BULLS DO NOT SEE RED
Bulls are color-blind, as are most animals. The bull charges when he sees a moving object, like a toreador's red cape. It is the movement of the cape, not the color, which angers the bull.

CAMELS DON'T STORE WATER IN THEIR HUMPS
Camels' humps are made of fat. They can travel for long periods in the desert without food because their bodies use the fat in the humps as nourishment. However, camels are able to drink great amounts of water, which is stored in their stomachs.

ELEPHANTS DON'T DRINK THROUGH THEIR TRUNKS
Elephants swallow food and liquids through their mouths. They use their trunks like straws, sucking up the liquid and spraying it into their mouths. At the end of their trunks are "fingerlike" muscles which they use to pick up food. Then they place the food in their mouths.

Life Spans of Animals

How long do animals live? The average human being lives to the age of 70+ years. Most animals do not live that long. For example, a 19-year-old horse is an old horse, but a 19-year-old human is considered young. Below is a list of common animal pets and their average life spans.

Animal	Average Life Span	Animal	Average Life Span
Cats	12 years	Horses	20 years
Dogs	12 years	Mice	3 years
Goats	8 years	Rabbits	5 years
Goldfish	7 years	Turtles (Box)	35 years
Guinea Pigs	4 years	Turtles (Slider)	15 years
Hamsters	2 years		

Where Animals Live

Animal	Common Name of Home	Animal	Common Name of Home
ant	hill	horse	
barnacle	shell	(domesticated)	barn
beaver	dam	lion	den
bee	hive	mole	hole
bird	nest	mule	shed
chicken		(domesticated)	or barn
(domesticated)	coop	rabbit	
clam	shell	(domesticated)	hutch
cow		spider	web
(domesticated)	barn	snail	shell
fox	hole		

Milk-Giving Animals of the World

The milk of animals is used by people everywhere for nourishment. Americans and Europeans commonly use cow's milk. Here are other animals whose milk is used by people.

Buffalo—Egypt, India, Pakistan
Camel—deserts of Africa and Asia
Donkey—China
Sheep—Greece

Horse—China
Reindeer—Lapland
Goat—Greece
Yak—Tibet

Animal Champions

MAMMALS

Largest*	**Blue Whale**	100 ft. long, 150 tons
Largest land animal	**African Bush Elephant**	10 ft., 6 in. tall, 6 tons
Smallest	**Kitti's Hog-nosed Bat**	1½ to 3 grams
Fastest	**Cheetah**	70 miles per hour
Slowest	**Three-toed Sloth**	6 to 8 ft. per minute (1/10 mile per hour)
Best jumper, longest jumper	**Kangaroo**	Jumps up to 10½ ft. high, 30 feet in distance
Longest breathholder	**Bottle-nosed Whale**	Can stay underwater 2 hours without air

The Blue Whale is the largest of all animals, living or extinct.

BIRDS

Largest	**Ostrich**	8 ft. tall, 300 pounds
Largest flying	**Wandering Albatross**	12-foot wingspan, 26 pounds
Smallest	**Bee Hummingbird (Cuba)**	2 inches head to tail, 1/10 ounce
Highest flying	**Bar-headed Goose**	29,000 ft. high
Fastest flying	**Indian Swift**	200 miles per hour, diving
Fastest gliding	**Vulture**	90 miles per hour
Deepest diver	**Emperor Penguin**	885 feet below water surface

FISH

Largest	**Whale Shark**	100 ft. long, 13 tons
Largest freshwater	**Pirarucu**	15 ft. long, 500 pounds
Smallest	**Dwarf Goby**	Less than ½ inch long (4 milligrams)
Fastest	**Sailfish**	68 miles per hour
Slowest	**Seahorse**	10½ inches per minute
Most electric	**Electric Eel**	400 volts

REPTILES

Largest	**Saltwater Crocodile**	16 ft. long, 1,150 pounds
Smallest	**Gecko**	Less than ¾ inch long
Fastest	**Leatherback Turtle**	22 miles per hour
Slowest	**Tortoise**	15 ft. per minute
Largest Snake	**Anaconda**	37 ft. long, 1,000 pounds
Largest poisonous snake	**King Cobra**	18 feet long
Fastest snake	**Black Mamba**	7 miles per hour

INSECTS

Largest	**Atlas Moth**	10-inch wingspan
Heaviest	**Goliath Beetle**	¼ pound
Fastest	**Dragon Fly**	36 miles per hour
Best jumper	**Flea**	Can jump 7¾ inches high, 13 inches in distance

Animals—Which Is Which?

ASSES, DONKEYS, AND MULES

The ass and the donkey are both members of the horse family. An ass lives in the wild; a donkey is a domesticated ass that has been selectively bred by people. A mule is a completely different animal because it is a cross between a horse and a donkey.

DOLPHINS AND PORPOISES

Both dolphins and porpoises belong to the whale order, but dolphins are generally larger than porpoises. They are mammals, not fish. Dolphins have long beaklike snouts; porpoises have blunt snouts. Dolphins are probably the most playful group of whales.

KANGAROOS AND WALLABYS

The only difference between a kangaroo and a wallaby is foot size. A wallaby is a medium-sized kangaroo with 10-inch hind feet. A kangaroo's hind feet are more than 10 inches long.

RABBITS AND HARES

Hares are larger than rabbits. Their hind feet and ears, in particular, are longer than those of rabbits. A hare is born with fur and with its eyes open. When a rabbit is born, its skin does not yet have hair, and its eyes are temporarily closed. Except for cottontail rabbits, all American wild rabbits are hares.

RATS AND MICE

Rats are many times larger than mice and have hairless tails; mice have hairy tails. A common mouse is 3½ to 4 inches long with a 2- to 3-inch tail. Rats have, on average, a 7- to 10-inch body with a 5- to 8-inch tail.

SEALS AND SEA LIONS

Fur seals and sea lions belong to the same animal family, and they have external ears. A type of seal, the true seal, has no external ears. Also, fur seals have more body hair than sea lions. The seals that perform in circuses are actually sea lions.

?

SHEEP AND GOATS
A sheep's tail hangs down. A goat's tail stands up. A male goat (a billy) usually has a beard (called a "goatee"). A male sheep (a ram) does not. Sheep "mind their own business" and are conformists. Goats are unpredictable and more aware of what's going on around them.

TURTLES, TORTOISES, AND TERRAPINS
In a general sense, all of these reptiles can be called turtles. Turtles that live on land all the time are called tortoises; freshwater turtles that are edible are called terrapins. All other freshwater and saltwater species are called turtles.

Famous Animals in History

"BARRY," THE CANINE HERO
This Saint Bernard saved 41 lives over a period of 12 years. Barry was kept at the Hospice of Saint Bernard, near a dangerous pass in the Swiss Alps. He had an exceptional ability to find and rescue people who were lost in sudden severe snowstorms. Barry died in 1814 at the age of 14. His body was preserved and now stands in a glass case in the Museum of Natural History in Berne, Switzerland.

"BLACK JACK," THE SYMBOL OF A FALLEN LEADER
When U.S. President John Kennedy was assassinated in 1963, Black Jack was chosen as the riderless horse for the funeral parade. Black Jack walked behind the casket, wearing an empty saddle with riders' boots reversed in the stirrups. This symbolized a leader had fallen and would never ride again.

Black Jack died in 1976 at the age of 29. Because he was the last of his kind, a U.S. Army Quartermaster-issue horse with an army brand on his shoulder and an army serial number on his neck, he was buried in the parade ground of Saint Myer's Summeral Field in Virginia.

"COMANCHE," THE SOLE SURVIVOR OF CUSTER'S LAST STAND
U.S. General George Custer's 7th Cavalry was defeated by the Sioux Indian tribe in the Battle of Little Big Horn in 1876. Comanche, a cavalry horse, was the army's only survivor.

"IGLOO," THE FIRST DOG TO FLY OVER NORTH AND SOUTH POLES
Admiral Richard Byrd took his pet fox terrier, Igloo, with him when he was first to fly over the South Pole in 1926 and the North Pole in 1928.

"JUMBO," WORLD FAMOUS ELEPHANT
Jumbo became famous as a P.T. Barnum circus elephant. He was billed as the "largest elephant in or out of captivity." Jumbo, who was 11 feet tall and weighed 6½ tons, introduced a new word to the English language. His name, Jumbo, came to mean anything of great size. When he died in 1885, it was estimated that Jumbo had given rides to over a million children in his lifetime.

"LAIKA," THE SPACE TRAVELER
Laika, a female Samoyed husky, was the first "animalnaut" to orbit the earth. In November 1957, Laika was sent into space in a satellite by the Soviets. Because they were then incapable of bringing the satellite back to earth, Laika was painlessly put to death by remote control.

"MARENGO," NAPOLEON'S FAVORITE HORSE
Marengo was a white Arabian stallion who carried the French Emperor, Napoleon, through many battles. In doing so, Marengo was wounded eight times. When Napoleon was defeated in his final battle at Waterloo in 1815, he was riding Marengo. Taken as a prize of war, Marengo's skeleton is on display today in the National Army Museum in London, England.

"MARTHA," THE LAST PASSENGER PIGEON
Twenty-six-year-old Martha, the last of her species, died in 1914 at the Cincinnati Zoo. She is now on exhibit at the Smithsonian Institution in Washington, D.C. Passenger pigeons once existed in great numbers in the eastern U.S. They were hunted to extinction because of their popularity as food.

Animal Mascots for the U.S. Military

MARINES:
Bulldog

The U.S. Marines wanted a tough-looking dog for a mascot. During World War I, the German soldiers said the Marines fought like "devil dogs." Devil dogs are the name of fierce dogs of German Bavarian folklore. The Marines chose the English bulldog as a mascot because it looks as tough as they are.

NAVY:
Goat

Goats have long been the pets of sailors. In 1893, at the fourth Army-Navy football game, the Naval Academy first paraded a goat as their mascot.

AIR FORCE:
Falcon

In 1955, the first Air Force Academy class selected the falcon as their mascot. The falcon represents the character of the Air Force because of its speed, keen eyesight, alertness, graceful flight, courage, and noble carriage. The official name of the falcon mascot is Mach One.

ARMY:
Mule

The U.S. Military Academy at West Point chose the mule as its mascot because the mule had been a longtime army packhorse and soldier's helper. George Washington, the first U.S. Army general, was also the first to breed mules in America.

Mistaken Identities Of Animals

A PANDA IS NOT A BEAR

There are two kinds of pandas. The Giant Panda is a big, black-and-white animal which looks like a bear. The Lesser Panda is smaller, has reddish-brown fur, and looks more like a raccoon. They are closely related, but scientists do not agree on how to classify them. Some scientists put them in the raccoon family; some put only the Giant Panda in the bear family. Most give both pandas a classification of their own.

A PONY IS NOT A BABY HORSE
Ponies are a separate, smaller breed of horse. Grown ponies never reach the size of standard horses. Three pony breeds are Shetland, Welsh, and Highland.

A PRAIRIE DOG IS NOT A DOG
Prairie dogs are rodents and are closely related to squirrels. They were named for their "barking" sound, which resembles a dog's bark.

A SPANISH FLY IS NOT A FLY
A Spanish fly is actually a beetle. It is also called a "blister beetle" because touching it causes burning pain and skin blisters.

THE SILKWORM IS NOT A WORM
The silkworm is an Asian Moth, *Bombyx mori*. Before becoming a moth, it is a yellow, hairless caterpillar, producing silk when it constructs its cocoon.

Mealtime at the Bronx Zoo

A great deal has been written about what animals eat in the wild. But have you ever wondered what they are fed at the zoo? The daily diet of five mammals at the Bronx Zoo, Bronx, New York, is listed below.

GIANT ANTEATER 1¼ pounds of horsemeat, 1 pound milk, ¼ pound of egg yolks.

GORILLA ½ pound of primate diet (a mix of grain, eggs, milk, minerals, vitamins, and other foods), ½ pound Monkey Chow (a mix of grain, meats, vitamins, minerals, and other foods), 4 carrots, 1 egg, 4 oranges, 1 yam, 3 apples, 2 bananas, ½ bunch of celery, ½ head of lettuce, 6-10 grapes, ⅛ pound of horsemeat, grass.

INDIAN ELEPHANT 28 pounds of D&H (a mix of grain products), 4 pounds of apples, 4 pounds of carrots, 4 pounds of potatoes, 14 pounds of hydroponic grass (oats and barley), 4 bales of timothy hay.

POLAR BEAR	1¼ pounds of apples, 1¼ pounds of chicken backs, 3 pounds of mackeral, 15 pounds of Bear Chow, 1½ pounds of hydroponic Grass (oats and barley).
SEA LION	10 pounds of mackeral, vitamin supplement

Odd Facts About Animals

• **Dolphins** sleep with one eye open at all times.

• **Domestic cats**, which first appeared in Egypt in 2500 B.C., were considered sacred. When they died, they were mummified as a sign of love and respect.

• **Polar bears** have hair on the soles of their feet to keep them from slipping on the ice.

• A **gorilla** will stick its tongue out to show anger.

• The **toucan** is a South American bird with a colorful beak. When it sleeps, it is able to turn its head almost all the way around and rest its beak on its back.

• **Sea worms** are the most numerous creatures on earth. They number an estimated 40 septillion.

• A **wild turkey** is capable of flying at a speed of 55 miles per hour.

• The **horseshoe crab** is the only animal to chew its food with its legs.

• The **hummingbird** is the only bird that can fly backwards. Like a helicopter, it is also able to fly up and down, and it can hover in midair.

• The **pig** is the only mammal other than man that can get sunburned.

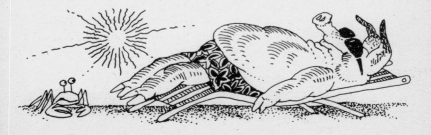

About Dogs

• The **Basenji**, an African breed, is the only kind of dog that does not bark. It is a curly-tailed, chestnut-brown dog.

• The **Saint Bernard**, the heaviest breed of dog, has an average weight of 170 pounds.

• The **Chihuahua**, the smallest breed of dog, usually weighs one to six pounds.

• The **Irish Wolfhound** is the tallest breed of dog, standing 30 to 34 inches at the shoulder.

• The **Greyhound**, a racing dog, is the fastest breed of dog. Greyhounds have been timed at speeds of up to 40 miles per hour.

Animal Extinction and Endangerment

Since life began, thousands of animal species have come and gone. Dinosaurs, for example, no longer exist because of the natural process of extinction. In the last few hundred years, however, animal extinction has increased at an alarming rate. People have hunted some animals to extinction; they have polluted the environment, and they have destroyed animal habitats in order to use them as their own. Consequently, some experts estimate the rate of extinction will increase to one extinct species a minute by 1990.

There is no way to bring back extinct animals, but endangered animals can be protected so that they will not become extinct. In 1973, the U.S. government passed a law called the Endangered Species Act to protect endangered animals. The following is a list of the questions the government asks to determine if an animal is endangered:

1. Is the birth rate lower than the death rate?
2. Can the animal adapt to changes in the environment?
3. Is the animal's living space (land, water, air) being destroyed?
4. Is the animal being harmed by pesticides and industrial wastes?
5. Is the animal threatened by disease, competition, or overhunting by other animals?

If the answer to one or more of these questions is Yes, the animal is placed on the endangered list.

Measures are taken to help the animal by breeding, banning chemicals, and restoring habitats. The following is only a partial list of the many animals of the world on the endangered list.

AMPHIBIANS

Frog, Pine Barrens
Salamander, Desert Slender

Toad, Houston

BIRDS

Albatross, Short Billed
Blackbird, Yellow Shouldered
Bobwhite, Mashed
Condor, Andean
Crane, Whooping
Duck, Hawaiian
Eagle, Bald

Falcon, American
Goose, Aleutian Canada
Parakeet, Paradise
Parrot, Puerto Rican
Pelican, Brown
Sparrow, Cable Sable Seaside
Stork, Wood Tern, Least

FISH

Chub, Humpback
Darter, Maryland

Pupfish, Warm Springs
Trout, Gila

MAMMALS

Bat, Indiana
Bear, Brown
Cheetah
Chimpanzee
Deer, Marsh
Elephant, Asian, African
Gorilla
Jaguar
Kangaroo, Tasmanian
Leopard, Snow
Lion, Asiatic Manatu, West Indian

Monkey, Black Howler
Otter, Southern Sea
Prairie Dog, Mexican
Rhinoceros, Black
Seal, Hawaiian Monk
Sloth, Brazilian Three-toed
Squirrel, Delmarva Peninsula Fox
Whale, Blue, Sperm, and Gray
Wolf, Gray
Yak, Wild
Zebra, Mountain

REPTILES

Alligator, American
Crocodile, American
Lizard, Blunt-nosed Leopard

Snake, San Francisco Garter
Tortoise, Galapagos
Turtle, Green Sea

Dinosaurs

Facts About Dinosaurs

• Dinosaurs first appeared about 200 million years ago. The last ones died about 65 million years ago.

• Dinosaur fossils have now been found on every continent, including Antarctica.

• More dinosaur bones have been found in Canada than anywhere else in the world. In Dinosaur Provincial Park near Calgary, more than 200,000 bones, making 300 skeletons of more than 30 kinds of dinosaurs, have been unearthed.

• The world's "newest" dinosaur discoveries are the **Ultrasaurus (Ultralizard)** and **Supersaurus**, both thought to be more than five stories high.

Five Lesser Known Dinosaurs

• **Heterodontosaurus** (different-toothed lizard): This plant-eating dinosaur had three different kinds of teeth. These dinosaurs inhabited South Africa about 200 million years ago.

• **Kentrosaurus** (prickly lizard): Plates and spikes along its back, tail, and on its hind legs protected this plant-eating dinosaur of 140 million years ago.

• **Mussaurus** (mouse lizard): This dinosaur measured about eight inches in length. It was thought to have lived 200 million years ago in Argentina.

• **Parasaurolophus** (another rigid reptile): Known for its hollow crest which was thought to amplify sound, this dinosaur lived 70 million years ago.

• **Styracosaurus** (spike lizard): A plant-eating dinosaur with a bony, spike-edged neck frill that lived in Canada 70 million years ago.

What Happened to the Dinosaurs?

Scientists of today know a great deal about dinosaurs—what they looked like, how they lived, and when they lived. However, no one knows for sure why all the dinosaurs died. Below are some of the theories of dinosaur extinction.

EXPLODING STAR

An exploding star might have started a heat wave which made the earth's weather too hot for life to survive. Also, radiation from the exploding star might have killed the dinosaurs or prevented them from having babies.

METEORITES

Large meteorites may have bombarded the earth, throwing up clouds of dust and blocking out the sun for a long period of time. The earth chilled, and dinosaurs could not live in the cold environment.

VOLCANOES

Extreme volcanic activity may have destroyed the earth's protective ozone layer, which lies between the earth's atmosphere and outer space. Too much deadly ultraviolet radiation from the sun would have then reached the earth and killed the dinosaurs.

GRADUAL EXTINCTION

A combination of events could have caused a slow, not a sudden, extinction of dinosaurs. Among the possible events: temperature and sea-level changes, migration, and the spread of disease among dinosaurs.

Fantastical Animals

Animals of fantasy and myth were created by people to tell stories and to explain the mysteries of life. These fabled creatures of long ago still excite children and grownups of the modern world. Some of the most memorable fantastical animals are listed and described below.

CENTAUR   Part-horse, part-man, the centaurs were savage creatures who represented the wild and lawless behavior of humans.

CHIMERA   This fire-breathing beast had a lion's head, a goat's body, and a serpent's tail. A mountain dweller, her fiery breath was said to be the reason for volcanic eruptions.

DRAGONS   These enormous, lizardlike creatures breathed fire. They liked to steal treasure, which they then guarded jealously. European dragons were said to represent the evil of humans; Asian dragons brought wealth and good luck.

GRIFFINS, GRYPHONS	These fabulous animals had an eagle's head and wings and a lion's body. Griffins guarded the sun and its hidden treasures.
MERMAIDS, MERMEN	Half-human and half-fish, mermaids and mermen lured sailors to their deaths under the sea with their singing.
PEGASUS	This legendary winged horse was given to Prince Bellerophon to help him conquer the Chimera.
PHOENIX	A fabulous bird with gold and purplish feathers. In Egyptian myth, the Phoenix sacrificed itself to fire and arose, reborn, from its own ashes.
SATYRS	In Greek mythology, these half-men, half-goats were associated with music and merriment.
SIRENS	Half-woman, half-bird, the sirens lived on rocky shores and lured sailors to their death with their mournful singing. The sirens were thought to be the unhappy souls of the dead who envied the living.
UNICORN	The unicorn had a horse's head and body, a deer's legs, a lion's tail, and a single horn in the middle of its forehead. This mythical animal represented purity. The horn also had the power to detect and purify poison.

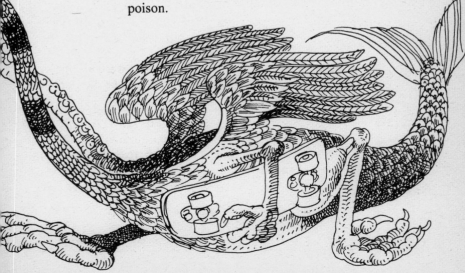

Body and Health

If you would like to know about bruises, bumps, growing pains, and growling stomachs, this is the chapter for you! It's also filled with facts on that very complex machine—the human body. And for keeping that machine healthy, there is a list of fitness foods that are fun to eat.

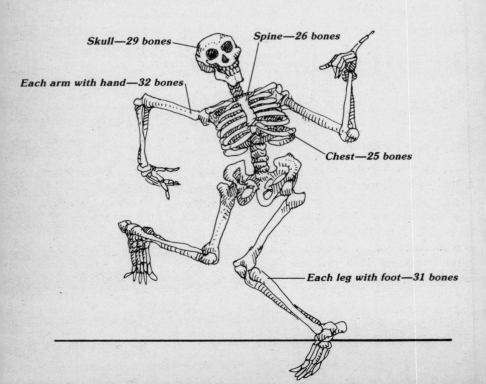

Skull—29 bones

Spine—26 bones

Each arm with hand—32 bones

Chest—25 bones

Each leg with foot—31 bones

Body Facts

Bones

• The largest bone is the femur, or thigh bone, which is 20 inches in a six-foot-tall man.
• The smallest bone is the stirrup in the ear, which is one-tenth of an inch.
• Each hand has 27 bones: eight in the wrist, five in the palm, and 14 in the fingers.
• A newborn baby has 300 bones, some of which fuse to form 206 in the adult.

Blood

• In a child, there are 60,000 miles of blood vessels.
• An adult has 100,000 miles of blood vessels.
• The blood circulates through the body 1,000 times a day.

Brain

• A newborn baby has a brain that weighs three ounces.
• The average brain of an adult weighs three pounds.
• The brain is the "mission control center" of the body, sending out messages at a rate of 240 miles per hour.
• The left side of the brain controls the right side of the body and the right side of the brain controls the left side of the body.

Cells

• The cells are the body's building blocks.
• There are about 26 billion cells in a newborn baby.
• There are about 50 trillion cells in an adult.

Eyes

• Each eye weighs 1¼ ounces.
• The eyes are constantly in motion, even during sleep.
• Tears keep the eyes warm and clean and are continually secreted through 12 ducts in the eye. Tears are normally secreted through two canals near the inner corner of the eyes.

Fluid

• The body is two-thirds water. Blood is 83% water, muscles are 75% water, the brain is 74% water, and the bones contain 22% water.
• In a single day, three pints of saliva are produced in the mouth.

Hair

• Kids have about 75,000 hairs on their heads, which grow about 1/100 of an inch daily.
• Hairs of different colors grow at different rates. Dark hair grows faster than light-colored hair. No one knows why.
• Each hair on the scalp grows about five inches a year.
• Eyelashes keep dust out of the eyes. An eyelash lives about 150 days before it falls out and is replaced.

Muscles

• There are over 650 muscles in the body, from the tiny ones that move the eyelids to the powerful ones that move the legs.
• The strongest muscle is the masseter muscle of the jaw.
• It takes at least 14 muscles to smile.
• The smallest muscle in the body is located in the middle ear.
• Fingers have no muscles.

Nails

• Nails are made up of hardened skin called *keratin*. Nails protect the ends of the fingers and toes.
• The half-moon at the root of the nail is called the *lunule*.

• Nails grow faster in summer than in winter.
• Fingernails grow four times faster than toenails.
• Right-handed people's nails grow faster on their right hands. Left-handed people's nails grow faster on their left hand.

Nose

• More than 2,500 gallons of air flow through the average adult's nose in a day.
• The nose can recognize up to 1,000 different smells.
• The nose is the air conditioning unit of the body. It cools or warms incoming air. It also filters the dirt and dust in the air.

Skin

• The human body has six pounds of skin which is, on average, 1/20 of an inch thick.
• The two layers of skin are the epidermis and, under it, the dermis.
• The skin is waterproof; it protects the body and helps to regulate body temperature.
• A substance called *melanin* colors the skin. The more melanin, the darker the skin. A freckle is a dense concentration of melanin.
• A new layer of skin replaces the old layer approximately every 27 days, totaling about 1,000 new outer layers of skin in a lifetime.

Teeth

• Humans have 20 primary (baby) teeth and 32 permanent teeth. By age 13 most people have 28 teeth. By age 18 the four "wisdom" teeth have usually grown in for a total of 32 permanent teeth.

• Teeth are shaped differently in order to chew food. The front teeth (incisors) are sharp and cut food. The cuspids and bicuspids break it up, and the molars grind it.

Name of Tooth	Age it Appears
(UPPER TEETH)	
central incisor	*7-8 years*
lateral incisor	*8-9 years*
cuspid	*11-12 years*
first bicuspid	*10-11 years*
second bicuspid	*10-12 years*
first molar	*6-7 years*
second molar	*12-13 years*
third molar	*17-21 years*
(LOWER TEETH)	
third molar	*17-21 years*
second molar	*11-13 years*
first molar	*6-7 years*
second bicuspid	*11-12 years*
first bicuspid	*10-12 years*
cuspid	*9-10 years*
lateral incisor	*7-8 years*
central incisor	*6-7 years*

Body Signs

Black and Blue Mark (Bruise)

When a blow to the body damages capillaries (the smallest blood vessels), blood leaks and collects in the skin tissue. As the bruise heals, the color of the blood changes from red to purple to blue to green to yellow.

Blackhead   A skin pore that is clogged with oils. The black color is not dirt but secretions of skin glands clogged in the pore.

Bump   A blow to the body where the skin is tight, particularly near a bone, causes a bump. The accumulation of plasma and blood cells causes the skin to swell where the skin is tight.

Blush   The brain triggers the dilation (expansion) of tiny capillaries near the surface of the skin. Blood fills the capillaries and the skin reddens. A feeling of embarrassment may cause a person to blush.

Canker Sore   An ulcer or sore in the mouth caused by injury or, more commonly, by a virus.

"Charley Horse"   A cramp or tightening of the muscle caused by stress on that muscle.

Dandruff   Loose flakes of dead skin cells of the scalp. Dandruff is very common and is usually due to dryness of the scalp, but it can also result from a fungus infection or a skin disease.

Funny Bone   The spot on the back of elbow, near the bone, where the ulnar nerve, which runs the arm's length, rests against the *humerus*. A blow to that spot hits the nerve and tingles.

Goose Bumps   Small muscles under the skin's surface contract and make the hairs stand up, causing small bumps. Goose bumps are the body's way of keeping warm.

Growing Pains   There is no such thing. However, kids often have pain in their joints and limbs at night from muscle fatigue.

Hangnail   Loose skin that hangs at the side or root of the fingernail.

Pimple   A small infection of a clogged oil gland at the base of the hair shaft in the skin.

Scab   When the skin is cut, clotted blood forms around the cut to close it. The clot forms a crust, or scab. When the skin tissue heals, the scab falls off.

Scar   When a wound heals and the skin cells do not join together perfectly, the result is a scar.

Tension Headache   Tension in the neck and shoulders causes scalp muscles to contract. Nerve endings in the scalp react to the tightened muscles by sending a signal to the brain, which interprets the signal as pain.

Wart   A growth on the skin caused by a virus.

Writer's Finger   A callus or hardening of the skin caused by constant pressure from holding a pen or pencil.

Body Noises

Sound	Medical Term	Reason
Burp	Eructation	The stomach releases extra air that has been swallowed with food.
Gas	Flatulence	Swallowed air that does not escape as a burp moves through the intestines, where it picks up gases made by bacteria. The gas is then passed out of the rectum.
Hiccup, Hiccough	Singulthus	A spasm of the diaphragm. The diaphragm is a muscle that pushes air in and out of the lungs. When the rhythm of the disphragm is off, incoming air bumps against the flap at the back of the throat and causes a "hic" sound.
Sneeze	Stenutation	A clearing of the nose when it is irritated by dust, mucus, or a smell.

| Snore | — | A noisy breathing sound made by a sleeping person. It is caused by air vibrating against the uvula, at the back of the mouth. |

| Stomach Growl | Borborgymus | The sound of the stomach muscles churning air and liquid in an otherwise empty stomach. Or, more commonly, churned up liquid food moving through the intestines. |
| Yawn | Pandiculation | The exact cause is not known. Since a yawn brings in extra air, it is thought to result from the body's need for extra oxygen. |

A Doctor Directory

Allergist—Treats allergies.

Anesthesiologist—Puts patients to sleep before surgery.

Cardiologist—Treats heart ailments.

Dermatologist—Treats the skin and its diseases.

Endocrinologist—Treats the glands, such as the thyroid and adrenal, which secrete body hormones.

Gastroenterologist—Specializes in diseases and disorders of the digestive system.

Gerontologist—Treats diseases of old age.

Gynecologist—Treats the female reproductive system.

Hematologist—Treats blood diseases.

Immunologist—Specializes in the body's defense system against infection and disease.

Nephrologist—Treats kidney disorders.

Neurologist—Treats the nervous system.

Obstetrician—A doctor who cares for women throughout pregnancy.

Opthamologist—Treats the eye and its diseases.

Orthopedist—Treats disorders of bones and muscles.

Orthodontist—A dentist who specializes in straightening teeth.

Otolaryngologist—Treats ailments of the nose, throat, and ears.

Pathologist—Studies the cause, development, and manifestations of disease.

Pediatrician—Specializes in the care and treatment of infants and children.

Plastic Surgeon—Repairs, restores, or improves body parts.

Psychiatrist—Treats illness and disorders of the mind.

Radiologist—X-rays body parts and organs for medical diagnosis.

Rheumatologist—Treats diseases of body joints.

Urologist—Treats the urinary tract of the body.

Fun Foods for Fitness

FOR FRESH BREATH	Chew **parsley,** which contains chlorophyll, a natural breath freshener.
FOR DIGESTION	**Bread crusts** have more fiber than the rest of the loaf and fiber is important to digestion.
	Popcorn adds roughage, which aids in digestion.
FOR STRONG TEETH	**Apples, carrots** and other crunchy fruits and vegetables need chewing, which increases the flow of saliva and cleans the teeth.
	Popcorn cleanses and massages the gums and teeth.
	Tea has a high fluoride content, which protects teeth from decay.

Eating **cheese** after a meal or snack may help prevent tooth decay. It is now thought that cheese may fight the bacteria in the mouth that causes cavities.

FOR QUICK ENERGY

Honey is a predigested food that gives energy without making your body work hard to digest it.

FOR THIRST

Water is the best thirst quencher and health drink. Water carries nutrients and oxygen to body tissues, lubricates your joints, and cools your body through perspiration. Soft drinks do not quench thirst because they contain salt, sugar, and caffeine, which raise your body's need for water.

FOR WEIGHT CONTROL

Grapefruit is low in calories and, when eaten, causes the release of a hormone, cholecystokinin, which suppresses the appetite. However, it is not a good idea to eat only grapefruit if you're on a diet, since it does not supply all of the nutrients the body needs each day.

Books

"Bookworms" take heed! There are real worms out there that gobble up books! Read about them and other tasty tidbits from the world of books. Meet some of your favorite authors and find out why they write for kids. Impress your friends with fancy words for bookish people. And for the real bookworm in you, check out the list of 50 popular books for kids as well as the top ten bestsellers of all time.

Bookish People

Biblioclast—Someone who destroys books.

Biblioklept—Someone who steals books.

Bibliomaniac—Someone who has an exaggerated love of books.

Bibliopegist—Someone who binds books; a bookbinder.

Bibliophage—Someone who reads a lot of books.

Bibliophile—Someone who loves books.

Bibliophobe—Someone who doesn't like books.

Bibliopole—Someone who sells rare books.

Bibliotaph—Someone who hoards books.

The Written Word

STYLES OF WRITING

Almanac   A book of general information including historical facts, records, weather information, and a calendar. Also, a yearbook on a certain subject, such as sports.

Anthology   A collection of writings, usually by many writers.

Atlas   A book of maps and geographical information tables.

Autobiography   The story of a person's life written by the same person.

Biography   The life history of a person, written by someone other than that person.

Diary   A day-to-day written record of events, thoughts, feelings, and personal activities.

"Dime Novels"   Popular American fiction published in a series and sold for a dime. The first true dime novels appeared in 1860 with "Beadle's Dime Novels."

Epic   A long poem telling the story of great heroes, real or legendary. Also, a novel or play that resembles this kind of poem.

Fable   A teaching story in which animals speak and act like humans. The lesson of a fable is found in the *moral* at the end of the story.

Fairy Tale   A story of the adventures of supernatural beings, such as fairies, goblins, and wizards.

Haiku   An unrhymed Japanese poem of three lines and containing 17 syllables (5,7, and 5, in that order). Haiku often refer to the seasons.

Journal   A day-by-day account of events and observations— usually less intimate then a diary.

Limerick
Humorous or light verse of five lines. Lines one, two, and five have 3 beats, and lines three and four have 2 beats.

EXAMPLE:
There was an old Man of the Dee,
Who was sadly annoyed by a Flea;
When he said, "I will scratch it,"
They gave him a hatchet,
Which grieved the old Man of the Dee.
—EDWARD LEAR, 1846

Nursery rhyme
A short rhyme for children that often tells a story.

Novel
A fictional story that tells of human experience through a sequence of events.

Saga
Originally a story of real or legendary heroes of Norway and Iceland. Today, it is a long, detailed account of events.

Book Notes

• A **bookworm** is not only a person who likes to read books. It is also an insect larva that feeds on the paste and bindings of a book.

• The **largest dictionary** in the world is the *Oxford English Dictionary.* It consists of 15,487 pages in 12 volumes.

• The **longest sentence** written in a novel is in *Absalom, Absalom!*, a novel by the American author William Faulkner. There are 1,300 words in the sentence.

• The **first book club** established in the U.S. was the Book-of-the-Month Club. It was started in 1926 with 4,750 members.

• The **first cookbook** printed in the world was published in Italy in 1475. Platina, a Vatican librarian, wrote the book and titled it *Concerning Honest Pleasure and Well Being.* The instructions for cooking larks' tongues and hummingbird livers are among the recipes.

• The **Encyclopedia Britannica** was first printed in England in 1771. Three Scotsmen, Andrew Bell, Colin Macfarquhar, and William Smellie compiled this distinguished book of information. Now in its fourth edition, the *Britannica* is the oldest continually published reference book in the English language.

• **An American Dictionary of the English Language** was published in two volumes by Noah Webster in 1828 after many years of study. He studied 26 languages to find the origin of the 70,000 words in his American dictionary. Webster "Americanized" the spelling of many words. For example, he changed the British spelling of *colour* to the American spelling *color.*

The Parts of a Book

Binding	The cover and fastenings that hold a book together.
Bibliography page	A list of writings by the author of the book, or a list of works by other authors on the same topic.
Book jacket	A removable paper cover used to protect the binding of a book.
Copyright page	The page listing the publication date, publisher, ISBN (International Standard Book Number), and Library of Congress catalog number.
Dedication page	A note in the book dedicating it to someone as a token of the author's esteem for that person.
Index	An alphabetized list of subjects and the page numbers where they can be found in the book.
Preface	A statement by the author introducing the book.
Spine	The supporting, rounded part of the book to which the covers are attached. It's the part you see when you look at a book in a bookcase.
Table of Contents	A list of chapters in the book.

Pen Names

(REAL NAMES OF FAMOUS AUTHORS)

Pen Name	Real Name	Books
Lewis Carroll	Charles Lutwidge Dodgson	*Alice's Adventures in Wonderland; Through the Looking Glass*
Robert C. O'Brien	Robert Leslie Conly	*Mrs. Frisby and the Rats of NIMH*
Richard Saunders	Benjamin Franklin	*Poor Richard's Almanac*
Dr. Seuss	Theodore Seuss Geisel	*The Cat in the Hat; The Grinch Who Stole Christmas; The Butter Battle Book,* etc.
Mark Twain	Samuel Langhorne Clemens	*Huckleberry Finn; Tom Sawyer*

Young Authors

• **Daisy Ashford** wrote *The Young Visitors,* a humorous novel about Victorian society, at the age of nine. She gave up writing when she was thirteen years old. *The Young Visitors* was published in 1919 in England, where it became a bestseller. Daisy (Margaret Mary) Ashford was born in England in 1881 and died in 1972.

• **Dorothy Straight** of Washington, D.C., is the youngest-known published author. She wrote *How the World Began* when she was four years old. In 1964, when she was six, her book was published by Pantheon Books of New York.

• **Benjamin Freedman** wrote and illustrated *The Ridiculous Book* when he was nine years old. The book was published in San Francisco by Pee Wee Press in 1978.

• **Allen Dulles** was eight when he wrote *The Boer War: A History*. Today the book is part of the rare books collection of the Library of Congress. Allen Dulles was a director of the CIA from 1953 to 1961. He was born in 1893 and died in 1969.

• **S.E. Hinton,** a popular American writer of teenage novels, published her first book, *The Outsiders,* when she was 17 years old.

Ten Authors for Children

LOUISA MAY ALCOTT.

Louisa May Alcott, the author of *Little Women, Little Men, Eight Cousins* and other popular books, was born in Germantown, Pennsylvania, in 1832. Her family was poor, and she and her sisters had to work at an early age to help with living expenses. Her most famous book, *Little Women,* was based on recollections of her own childhood. The four "little women" are portraits of herself and her three sisters, May, Elizabeth, and Anna. *Little Women* was published when Louisa was thirty-six years old. The book was very popular and earned Louisa enough money to pay her family's debts.

JUDY BLUME.

This popular author was born as Judy Sussman on February 12, 1938, in Elizabeth, New Jersey. She married John Blume and they had two children, a daughter, Randy Lee, and a son, Laurence Andrew. Today, Judy Blume lives in New York City and in Santa Fe, New Mexico. She uses the memories of her own youth in her books. She had a happy childhood, but she often felt alone with her problems and her curiosity about the adult world. Some of her books are: *Tales of a Fourth Grade Nothing, Are You There God, It's Me, Margaret,* and *Superfudge.*

BEVERLY CLEARY.

Beverly Cleary was born in 1916 in McMinnville, Oregon. She lived there on a large farm until she was six years old, when her family moved to Portland, Oregon. She spent her school years in Portland, which is the locale of many of her books. As a youngster, she had trouble learning to read. She remembers being put into the "Blackbirds," the slow reading group of her first grade class. She wanted to read, but somehow could not until she was eight years old. Then she remembers reading with great pleasure. She wanted to read books about children in her neighborhood and books that would make her laugh.

As an adult, she worked as a children's librarian, then got married and moved to Oakland, California. She is the mother of twins.

Her books for children are not written as grown-up remembrances of her life as a child. They are instead the kinds of books she wanted to read as a child—books that would give children the pleasure of reading and make them laugh. Some of her books are: the *Ramona* books, *The Mouse and the Motorcycle,* and *Dear Mr. Henshaw.*

PAULA DANZIGER.
Paula Danziger was born on August 18, 1944, in Washington, D.C. Today, she lives in New York City and Woodstock, New York. She knew when she was in second grade that she wanted to be a writer. It was then that she created a whole town of imaginary playmates, people whom she brought to life with her "magic pencil."

Formerly a junior high school teacher, Paula Danziger is today a novelist for young adults. One of her most popular books is *The Cat Ate My Gymsuit.*

TOMIE DE PAOLA.
Author and illustrator, Thomas Anthony De Paola was born in Meriden, Connecticut, on September 15, 1932. He feels fortunate that he grew up before television. When he was a child, he listened to the radio and read many books. His young imagination was sparked by listening, reading, and games of make-believe. When he was in the first grade, he announced to his teacher that when he grew up, he was going to make picture books. He made his first book for his younger sister's seventh birthday.

Today, Tomie de Paola lives in Wilmot Flat, New Hampshire. He has worked as a professional artist, designer, and teacher. He is best known for the many books he has written and illustrated for children, among them *Pancakes for Breakfast* and *Oliver Button is a Sissy.*

KENNETH GRAHAME.
Kenneth Grahame was born in Edinburgh, Scotland, in 1859. His mother died when he was five, and he and his sister and two brothers were raised by their grandmother. As an adult, he worked as a banker and wrote stories on weekends, calling himself a "Sunday writer." He and his wife, Elspeth Thomson, had one son, Alastair, who was affectionately called "Mouse." Grahame's classic children's story, *The Wind in the Willows*, was written for Alastair. Kenneth Grahame died in 1932.

SHEL SILVERSTEIN.
Shelby Silverstein was born in 1932 in Chicago, Illinois. He is a cartoonist, composer, lyricist, folksinger, and writer. When he was twelve years old, he wanted to be a good baseball player and be popular with girls. But he couldn't play ball and he couldn't dance, so he drew pictures and wrote poetry and stories. As an adult, he never planned to write and draw for kids, but a close friend of his insisted that he should. One of his early books, *The Giving Tree*, was first rejected by an editor who thought it was not quite for children and not quite for adults. *The Giving Tree*, as well as many other books by Silverstein, are enjoyed by kids and adults alike.

WILLIAM STEIG.
The author of *Sylvester and the Magic Pebbles* and *Abel's Island* was born in New York City in 1907. Born into a family of artists, Steig also became an artist. His first children's book was published when he was sixty-one years old. His ideas for stories usually start with a picture image. They are then filled with the joy of life.

William Steig says that meeting the children for whom he writes is one of the great challenges of being an author for children.

JOHN STEPTOE.
Joe Steptoe is a young black writer who was born in Brooklyn, New York, in 1950. He wrote and illustrated his first book, *Stevie*, when he was seventeen years old. His books are filled with the kids and urban ghetto neighborhood he knew when he was young. John Steptoe has worked as a teacher and illustrator. He is married to Stephanie Douglas and has one daughter and one son.

LAURA INGALLS WILDER.
The author of the *Little House* books was born in 1867 in Pepin, Wisconsin, the setting for her first book, *The Little House in the Big Woods*. About her writings, she said, "I lived everything that happened in my books. It is a long story, filled with sunshine and shadow."

Laura Ingalls Wilder wrote a series of nine books about her childhood and marriage in pioneer America before she died in 1957.

Fifty Contemporary Classics
for Every Child
(COMPILED BY THE AMERICAN LIBRARY ASSOCIATION)

ALEXANDER, LLOYD
The Book of Three
Taran, an Assistant Pig-Keeper in the kingdom of Prydain, sets off on a dangerous journey to find a missing magic pig, Hen Wen, and save his beloved kingdom. This is the first of five books about Taran and Prydain.

BABBITT, NATALIE
Tuck Everlasting
A timeless fantasy about a family who has unwittingly drunk from a spring of life, and Winnie, an eleven-year-old girl who must make some life-and-death decisions after stumbling on their secret at the same time as a stranger with evil intentions.

BOND, MICHAEL
A Bear Called Paddington
A mischievous bear with a penchant for getting into trouble comes to live with the Brown family, who found him in Paddington Station, London.

BOND, NANCY
A String in the Harp
When Peter and his siblings are unwillingly moved to Wales, Peter discovers an ancient harp-tuning key that transports him back in time to the sixth-century world of the bard, Taliesin.

BOSTON, LUCY
The Children of Green Knowe
Tolly meets three lively children

who, in the 17th century, lived in the enchanted house of Green Knowe where Tolly has come to stay with his grandmother.

BYARS, BETSY C.
The Midnight Fox
The lively narrator tells a story about tracking a black fox during a summer on his uncle's farm.

CAMERON, ELEANOR
The Court of the Stone Children
While visiting a museum, Nina meets a girl who has come forward in time from the Napoleonic era and helps her solve a mystery begun in the 1700s.

CLEARY, BEVERLY
Ramona and Her Father
When her father loses his job, Ramona tries to help in her own unique—and ultimately funny—way.

CLEAVER, VERA AND BILL
Where the Lilies Bloom
A determined and resourceful fourteen-year-old maintains the independence of her orphaned family by gathering and selling medicinal herbs in the Appalachian mountain area where they live.

COLLIER, JAMES L. AND COLLIER, CHRISTOPHER
My Brother Sam is Dead
Impetuous and idealistic sixteen-year-old Sam defies his Tory father to join the Continentals in their war against the British in 1775.

COOPER, SUSAN
The Dark is Rising
The seventh son of a seventh son, eleven-year-old Will is irretrievably drawn into the eternal struggle between good and evil in this powerful fantasy set during the twelve days of Christmas.

CRESSWELL, HELEN
Ordinary Jack: Being the First Part of the Bagthorpe Saga
Jack Bagthorpe feels like a loser in a family of talented achievers. His Uncle Parker dreams up a scheme for Jack to win fame by becoming the family prophet—with broadly comic results.

DE JONG, MEINDERT
The House of Sixty Fathers
Through all of his encounters with Chinese guerrillas, Japanese invaders, and American airmen, a Chinese boy never gives up hope of finding his family in World War II occupied China.

DONOVAN, JOHN
Family
A group of laboratory apes escape to form a family in the wild until they are forced to throw themselves at the mercy of humankind.

FITZGERALD, JOHN D.
The Great Brain
Young John recalls the wheelings and dealings of his older brother, Tom, whose escapades continually keep their small Utah village in turmoil.

FITZHUGH, LOUISE
Harriet the Spy
The zany adventures of eleven-year-old Harriet, who learns more than she expects by keeping a secret notebook about family and friends.

FLEISCHMAN, SID
Humbug Mountain
In a rip-roaring tall tale set in the Old West, Wiley, Glorietta, and their parents outwit a crafty steamboat captain and rescue their grandfather from some nasty outlaws.

FOX, PAULA
Slave Dancer
A boy kidnapped from New Orleans in 1840 is forced to become the fife player on a slave ship and "dance" the human cargo for exercise—a realistic, moving story about the tragedy of slavery.

GREEN, BETTE
Summer of My German Soldier
In this sensitive novel set in a small southern town during World War II, a Jewish girl helps a German prisoner-of-war escape.

GREEN, CONSTANCE C.
Beat the Turtle Drum
Kate's world is turned upside down when her beloved young sister dies in a freak accident.

HOLMAN, FELICE
Slake's Limbo
Hounded by fear and misfortune, fifteen-year-old Slake retreats to a cave beneath New York's Grand Central Station, where he ingeniously survives for 121 days.

HUNTER, MOLLIE
A Stranger Came Ashore
The Selkie (seal) legend is woven into an exciting tale of a sealman's entrance into the lives of lovely Elspeth and her protective younger brother, Robbie.

KONIGSBURG, E.L.
From the Mixed-Up Files of Mrs. Basil E. Frankweiler
Narrated by rich, eccentric Mrs. Frankweiler, the story features Claudia and her brother who run away from home to the New York Metropolitan Museum of Art. There, they become involved in a mystery.

LANGTON, JANE
The Fledgling
In this well-plotted fantasy, eight-year-old Georgie learns to fly with the help of a great Canadian goose—but not without danger.

LE GUIN, URSULA K.
The Wizard of Earthsea
While learning to be a magician, Ged forgets that enchantment is not for entertainment and unleashes destructive forces which pursue him until he learns how to control them.

L'ENGLE, MADELEINE
A Wrinkle in Time
Determined to find their missing scientist father, Meg Murray, her brother, Charles Wallace, and Calvin O'Keefe accompany three extraterrestrials to an evil world in outer space.

LEWIS, C.S.
The Lion, the Witch and the Wardrobe
A spellbinding parable about four children who pass through an old English wardrobe into the magical land of Narnia, where they help Aslan, the lion ruler, free his subjects from the evil White Witch.

LIVELY, PENELOPE
The Ghost of Thomas Kempe
Young James Harrison must deal with the ghost of a 17th-century sorcerer who has returned to haunt his former home.

LOWRY, LOIS
Anastasia Krupnik
Anastasia worries about a new sibling and keeps a diary of things she hates and loves in this amusing tale about being ten.

MCKINLEY, ROBIN
Beauty: A Retelling of the Story of Beauty and the Beast
An elegantly-styled, romantic retelling of a classic fairy tale.

MATHIS, SHARON B.
The Hundred Penny Box
A one-hundred-year-old woman recalls people and places from her past as her sympathetic young grandnephew counts out pennies from her box, one for each year.

MERRILL, JEAN
The Pushcart War
A partly-comical, partly-serious tale of a war between the truck drivers and pushcart men on the streets of New York City.

NORTON, MARY
The Borrowers
A family of tiny people who live beneath the floors of a quiet country house and "borrow" the things they need enjoy a series of interesting adventures.

O'BRIEN, ROBERT C.
Mrs. Frisby and the Rats of NIMH
Alone in the world, a widowed mouse visits the rats whose former imprisonment in a laboratory has given them wisdom and long life.

O'DELL, SCOTT
Island of the Blue Dolphins
Nature becomes both friend and enemy to a young Indian girl as she struggles to survive on a deserted island.

PATERSON, KATHERINE
Bridge to Terabithia
Jess and Leslie, two unlikely friends, share an imagined world until tragedy strikes. A poignant story about friendship, sadness, and loss.

PECK, RICHARD
The Ghost Belonged to Me
This comic but hair-raising ghost story features a cast of individualistic characters in a turn-of-the-century midwestern town.

PINKWATER, DANIEL M.
Lizard Music
The zany adventures of a young sci-fi show addict who travels to an invisible island inhabited by charming lizards.

ROCKWELL, THOMAS
How to Eat Fried Worms
A ten-year-old hopes that worms taste delicious, since he has just made a bet that he'll eat 15.

RODGERS, MARY
Freaky Friday
Thirteen-year-old Annabel wakes up one morning to find that she and her mother have switched ages.

SELDEN, GEORGE
The Cricket in Times Square
Chester Cricket, transported in a picnic basket from rural Connecticut to Times Square, meets some surprising friends and is introduced to city life.

SNYDER, ZILPHA K.
The Egypt Game
Two imaginative children who share an enthusiasm for ancient Egypt find themselves involved in a neighborhood game that becomes more exciting than they ever expected.

SPEARE, ELIZABETH G.
The Witch of Blackbird Pond
Independent, attractive sixteen-year-old Kit comes to live with her aunt and uncle in Puritan Connecticut. When Kit is branded a witch by townspeople, she receives help from a handsome young sailor and a small child.

STEIG, WILLIAM
Abel's Island
The story of an elegant, leisure-loving mouse who gets swept away in a driving rainstorm and winds up stranded on a river island where he develops his soul as well as his survival skills.

WHITE, E.B.
Charlotte's Web
The life of Wilbur the pig is saved first by a tenderhearted girl named Fern and then by Charlotte, an extraordinary spider who weaves wonderful messages in her web.

WISEMAN, DAVID
Jeremy Visick
In this fantasy, Matthew travels back a century in time to help a boy his own age who was lost in a Cornish mining disaster.

YEP, LAURENCE
Dragonwings
This novel portrays two Chinese immigrants, a father and son, who adjust to working in America among "white demons," survive the 1906 San Francisco earthquake and struggle toward a dual dream of making an airplane and reuniting their family.

Ten Bestselling Children's Books Of All Time*

Title	Author	Publisher
The Tale of Peter Rabbit	Beatrix Potter	Frederick Warne
The Littlest Angel	Charles Tazewell	Children's Press
Real Mother Goose	—	Rand McNally
Pat the Bunny	Dorothy Kunhardt	Golden Books
The Children's Bible	—	Golden Books
Richard Scarry's Best Word Book Ever	Richard Scarry	Golden Books
The Very Hungry Caterpillar	Eric Carle	Philomel
The Cat in the Hat	Dr. Seuss	Random House
Green Eggs and Ham	Dr. Seuss	Random House
Winnie-the-Pooh	A.A. Milne	Dutton

*Source—The Book Publishing Annual, published by R.R. Bowker and Company

Buildings and Other Structures

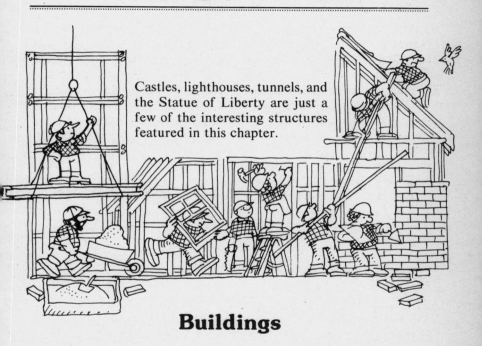

Castles, lighthouses, tunnels, and the Statue of Liberty are just a few of the interesting structures featured in this chapter.

Buildings

HOMES FROM A TO Z

Throughout history, people have built homes for shelter, comfort, and show. The many names of homes reflect their shape, size, location, building materials, or residents. Here, from A to Z, with the exception of X, are some of the names for structures which people call home.

Adobe—A house made from sun-dried bricks of clay and straw—usually built in warm, dry climates like the southwestern U.S.

Apartment—A set of rooms in a building which usually contains other similar sets of rooms.

Barracks—A building or set of buildings used to house soldiers.

Boardinghouse—A house in which rooms are rented and meals are served in a common dining room.

Bungalow—A small house with a low, wide roof and a porch. It is usually one story high.

Chalet—A mountain house with a wide, overhanging roof and exposed posts and beams. The style originated in Switzerland.

Château—From the French word for castle, a château is also a country home built to look like a French castle.

Condominium—An apartment building or multi-unit structure in which each unit is individually owned.

Convent—A home for nuns.

Cottage—A small country home or summer house used for vacations.

Duplex Apartment—An apartment with two floors of living space.

Duplex House—A house divided into two living units.

Estate—A large country house with separate buildings on a large tract of land.

Farmhouse—The dwelling for people who live and work on a farm raising animals or crops.

Flat—An apartment on one floor of a building.

Geodesic Dome—A partial sphere, curved or domed, made of lightweight materials.

High-rise—A tall apartment building.

Houseboat—A large, flat-bottom boat used as a home.

Hogan—A building made of logs and mud, used by the Navaho Indians.

Igloo—A house built by Eskimos of blocks of ice. The name means "hot house."

Jacal—A thatched hut made of intertwined branches and mud, built in Mexico.

Konah—A large home in Turkey.

Lodge—A house usually located in a remote place and used for hunting or skiing.

Loft—An apartment in a warehouse or business building.

Log Cabin—A small house made of unhewn timber.

Manse—In Scotland, a house in which a minister lives.

Mobile Home—A trailer used as a permanent home and made without a permanent foundation.

Motor Home—A traveling home built on the frame of a truck or bus.

Nissen Hut—A premade shelter with a semicircular arching roof of corrugated iron, and containing a cement floor.

Octagon House—A house with eight sides.

Palace—A large, grand building in which royalty live.

Penthouse—A large apartment located at the top of a building.

Quonset Hut—A premade, portable, circular hut made of metal and used by the U.S. Army.

Rectory—The house in which a Roman Catholic priest or Episcopal clergyman lives.

Shanty—A shack.

Sod House—A house made of bricks of sod, which is earth with grass and its roots. In the 19th century, these were built on the American prairie where there were no trees, just grassy land.

Studio Apartment—A one-room apartment with a kitchen and bathroom.

Tent—A portable house made of skins, canvas, or nylon.

Tepee, Tipi—A cone-shaped portable home made of buffalo skins and tree saplings, used by the American Indians of the Great Plains.

Tenement—A rundown, low-rent apartment building.

Underground House—An earth shelter built below the ground. The earth keeps the house warm in the winter and cool in the summer.

Villa—A large country or resort home.

Wigwam—A hut with a frame made of poles and covered with bark, rush mats, or hides, used by American Indians.

Yurt—A circular, portable hut used as a home by Asian shepherds. It is similar to the American wigwam.

Zareba—An African fort made of thorny bushes.

OFFICIAL HOMES FOR HEADS OF GOVERNMENT

Throughout the world, the elected head of government is given a residence to live in during his or her term of office. These houses are official homes and offices for government leaders. Following is a list of some of the countries that have names for their official homes.

Country	Name of Home	Head of Government	Location
Canada	"24 Sussex Drive"	Prime Minister	Ottawa
India	Rashtrapati-Bhavan	President	New Delhi
Ireland	Aras An Vachtarain	President	Dublin
Italy	Quiranale	President	Rome
Mexico	Los Pinos	President	Mexico City
Portugal	Palacio de Belem	President	Lisbon
Spain	Palacio de la Moncloe	Premier	Madrid

Country	Name of Home	Head of Government	Location
West Germany	Federal Chancellor's Office	Chancellor	Bonn
United Kingdom	# 10 Downing Street	Prime Minister	London
United States	The White House	President	Washington, D.C.

Five Facts About School Buildings

1. The first schoolhouses in the U.S. were made of logs and had dirt floors. The windows were covered with greased paper. Tables were built into the walls, and students faced the wall when working. A fireplace warmed the building in cold weather.

2. The oldest existing elementary schoolhouse on its original site is the Voorlezer School in Staten Island, New York. It was built in 1695 by the Dutch Church and served as a schoolhouse and home for the teacher until the late 1700s. Today it is a national historic landmark open to the public for visiting.

3. There are 798 one-room schoolhouses in operation in the U.S. today. Many of them are in Nebraska, which has a total of 354.

4. The first circular school building to be built in the U.S. was St. Patrick Central High School in Kankakee, Illinois. The two-story building is 200 feet in diameter and houses classrooms and a gymnasium. It was built in 1956.

5. The most public school buildings in the U.S. are in the state of California. It has 2,183 schools.

Structures as National Symbols

Some statues, towers, and buildings throughout the world are so famous, they have come to stand for the country in which they are located. The following is a list of some of these symbolic structures.

Country	Structure	Location
Australia	Sydney Opera House	Sydney
Brazil	Christ the Redeemer Statue	Rio de Janeiro
China	Great Wall	Northern China
Egypt	Pyramids	Giza
France	Eiffel Tower	Paris
Greece	Parthenon (temple)	Athens
Holland	Windmills	Kinderdijk
India	Taj Mahal (tomb)	Agra
Ireland	Blarney Stone	Cork
Italy	Leaning Tower of Pisa	Pisa
Japan	Imperial Palace	Tokyo
U.S.	Statue of Liberty	New York Harbor
U.S.S.R.	Kremlin	Moscow

FACTS ABOUT THE STATUE OF LIBERTY

1. The official name of the Statue of Liberty is "Liberty Enlightening the World."

2. The Statue of Liberty is twenty times life size. Its statistics are as follows:

   The figure is 151 feet, one inch high.
   The base is 65 feet high.
   The pedestal is 89 feet high.
   The statue stands 305 feet above the water.
   The mouth is three feet wide.
   The statue weighs 450,000 pounds (225 tons).
   Each eye is 2½ feet wide.

Each forefinger is 8 feet long with a nail that is 10 by 13 inches long.

3. The designer of the Statue of Liberty was a Frenchman, Frederic Auguste Bartholdi, (1834-1904). The steel skeleton was built by Gustave Eiffel, also built the Eiffel Tower in Paris, France. Bartholdi fashioned the face of the statue after his beloved mother, Charlotte. The arms of his girlfriend, Jeanne-Emilie Baheax de Puysieux, were the model for the statue's arms.

4. The seven spikes on the crown of the Statue of Liberty symbolize the seven continents and seven seas of the world.

5. The statue holds a tablet on which is inscribed July 4, MDCCLXXVI (1776), the date of American independence.

6. The statue was assembled and stands on Bedloes Island in New York Harbor, New York City. The island was named after its original Dutch owner. In 1956, the name was changed to Liberty Island.

7. The statue was a gift from the people of France to the people of the United States in honor of freedom and democracy.

8. It took many years to build and transport the Statue of Liberty, but it was officially dedicated and opened in 1886.

9. In the beginning, the U.S. government officially maintained the Statue of Liberty as a lighthouse.

10. Restoration of the Statue of Liberty began in 1984. Among other repairs, the torch and the wrought-iron bands holding the statue's "skin" to its frame were replaced. An elevator was also installed. The restoration was completed by July 4, 1986, the statue's 100th birthday.

Notable Lighthouses

For centuries, lighthouses have been built on islands, coastlines, and in water to serve as guides and warnings to ships at sea. These structures were first illuminated with bonfires of wood or coal. Later, oil and kerosene lamps were used. Today, most lighthouses use electricity to send powerful beams of light over the dark seas at night.

Lighthouses have traditionally served as homes for their keepers. Today, however, many lighthouses are not inhabited. For example, in the U.S., where there are 450 active lighthouses, only 33 of them are used as homes. The rest are operated by remote control or by electronic devices which activate the lights at dusk. Seven notable lighthouses are listed below:

PHAROS
The Pharos Lighthouse was one of the Seven Wonders of the Ancient World. Perhaps the largest lighthouse ever, it had a 100-square-foot base with a 400-foot tower. It was built on an island near Alexandria, Egypt, in the third century B.C. and guided ships for more than seven centuries. In A.D. 641, the Pharos lighthouse was destroyed by an earthquake.

EDDYSTONE
The Eddystone Lighthouse is located on a reef in the English Channel, 14 miles from Plymouth, England. This lighthouse has been celebrated in story and song because of its long and difficult history. First built in 1696, it was swept out to sea by a great storm in 1703. Rebuilt in 1706, it was destroyed by fire in 1756. It was once again rebuilt in 1756 and stood until 1878 when it was replaced by an updated fourth lighthouse, which still stands today.

BOSTON LIGHT
The first lighthouse in the U. S. was the Boston Light built on Little Brewster Island in Boston Harbor in 1716. Because of its strategic position, American and British troops fought over the lighthouse during the Revolutionary War. In 1781, at the end of the war, defeated British troops destroyed the Boston Light as an act of defiance. Rebuilt in 1783, the Boston Light was equipped with the first fog signal in a U.S. lighthouse. The fog signal was a cannon fired at regular intervals dur-

ing heavy fog. The Boston Light is an 89-foot stone tower which is still in operation today.

SANDY HOOK

The oldest surviving lighthouse in the U.S. is the 85-foot-high Hook Lighthouse on the New Jersey side of New York Harbor. The original tower, built in 1763, has never been destroyed and still stands today. During the Revolutionary War, the lantern of the lighthouse was destroyed, but the tower escaped damage.

CREAC'H D'OUESSANT

The light of the Creac'h d'Ouessant Lighthouse in Brittany, France, is the most powerful in the world. It has a light intensity of 490,500,000 candles.

SANKATY HEAD

The Sankaty Head Lighthouse, known as "Bright Eyes," has the longest-ranging light in the U.S. Its three-million-candlepower light is visible 29 miles away. "Bright Eyes" is located on Northwest Island, Massachusetts.

THE LITTLE RED LIGHTHOUSE

A small red lighthouse, built on the Hudson River under the George Washington Bridge in New York City, is no longer used as a lighthouse but remains standing. It has been named an historical landmark because it was the inspiration for a children's book, *The Little Red Lighthouse and the Great Gray Bridge* by H.H. Swift and Lyn Ward.

A Guide to Castles

Castles were homes and fortresses for kings, queens, and nobles of the Middle Ages. Built in Europe from the ninth to the fifteenth century, they symbolized power and wealth. In a time of frequent battling over land and power, the castle was an important means of protection. Often built on high land, castles were made of thick walls and surrounded by barriers, such as moats, in order to make them difficult to attack.

Although most castles were built over 500 years ago, they still bring to mind a sense of excitement, adventure, and intrigue. Today, many medieval castles are in ruins; those that remain have been turned into museums or hotels. Below is a brief guide to the parts of a castle.

BAILEY
The inner courtyard or space enclosed by the castle walls.

BARBICAN
A tower located at the gate or drawbridge.

BATTLEMENTS
Built on top of the walls surrounding the castle and on top of the towers, they were part solid and part open. The solid parts of the battlements, called merlins, protected the defenders. The open parts, called embrasures, were used by the defenders to shoot arrows at, or to drop stones or boiling liquids on their enemies.

DONJON
A castle tower which was the strongest and safest part of the castle. Also called a keep.

DRAWBRIDGE
A bridge that could be raised to close off entrance to the castle.

DUNGEONS
Prison cells often located in the basement of the donjon or keep.

GARDEROBE
The castle toilet. Built of stone, the garderobe worked on the same principal as latter-day outhouses.

KEEP

The strongest tower in the castle where the nobleman's family usually lived. Also called a donjon.

MOAT

A wide and deep ditch built around the castle, usually filled with water.

PORTCULLIS

A strong iron gate with spikes at the bottom that protected the castle entrance.

RAMPART

The walk or ledge on the inside of the battlements where the defenders stood.

Tunnels

Tunnels are underground passageways made by removing soil or rock. Tunnels are built through mountains, under water, and beneath crowded cities. In earlier times, tunnels were built for tombs and for warfare. Today, water, trains, and vehicles move through the tunnels of the world. Highlights in the history of tunnel building and other facts about tunnels are listed below.

THE PARTS OF A TUNNEL

Tunnel builders have special names for the parts of a tunnel. They are as follows:

Tunnel Part	Name
Top	Crown or Roof
Floor	Invert
Sides	Sidewalls
Entrances	Portals or Mouths

HISTORICAL HIGHLIGHTS
IN TUNNEL-BUILDING HISTORY

• Ancient Egyptian kings put thousands of slaves to work building pyramids and tunnels. During a king's lifetime, slaves dug a tunnel through the rock. When the king died, he was buried deep below the pyramid in a tomb at the end of the tunnel. One of these kings, Mineptah, had a tunnel built that went 350 feet into the side of a hill with a shaft leading down to another tunnel which extended 300 feet into his tomb. Mineptah ruled Egypt around 2100 B.C.

• Around 200 B.C., the Buddhists of India began digging the world's most beautiful and elaborate tunnels. Within the stone tunnels, shrines with pillars, roofs, and sometimes aisles were carved out of the solid rock. One tunnel, built at Ellora, India, was more than a mile long with 34 shrines. It was all cut with a hammer and a chisel.

• The ancient Romans were among the world's great tunnel builders. Many of their tunnels were built to carry water to Rome. Water-carrying tunnels are called aqueducts (from the Latin words *aqua*, meaning "water," and *ductus*, "act of leading"). The Roman aqueducts, begun in 312 B.C., were named after the officials who built them. The Aqua Marcia, which consisted of 51 miles of tunnels, was named for Marcius Rex. One advantage of the Roman system of water tunnels was that they hid the water supply from enemies in time of war.

• Secret tunnels were built under medieval castles as a means of escape in case the castle was in danger of being captured. Those attacking the castle often built tunnels to a castle corner where they set up beams. The beams were set afire. When the beams collapsed, the earth and walls above also collapsed, allowing the enemy to break through the opening into the castle.

NOTABLE MODERN TUNNELS

LONGEST RAILROAD TUNNEL
The Seikan Rail Tunnel in Japan is an undersea tunnel that is 33.5 miles long. It connects the island of Honshu to the island of Hokkaido under the Tsuguru Strait in the Pacific Ocean.

LONGEST AUTO AND TRUCK TUNNEL
The two-lane St. Gotthard Tunnel in Switzerland is 10.14 miles long. It passes through the Alps.

LONGEST SUBWAY TUNNEL
The Moscow Metro line running from Belyaevo to Medvedkovo is 19.07 miles long. It is the longest continuous tunnel of an underground railway.

LONGEST WATER TUNNEL
The Delaware Aqueduct, which supplies water to New York City, is 105 miles long.

SHORTEST U.S. TUNNEL
The Bee Rock Tunnel near Appalachia, Virginia, is a 30-foot-long railroad tunnel.

HIGHEST TUNNEL
The three-mile-long Galera Tunnel in the Andes Mountains of Peru is 15,655 feet or three miles above sea level at its highest point. The trains are equipped with oxygen for the passengers who have difficulty breathing at that height.

UNFINISHED TUNNEL
Often planned and once started, a tunnel under the English Channel has not been completed. The idea for a tunnel to link France and England under the English Channel was first suggested to the French emperor, Napoleon, as a means of invading England. During the 19th century, French and English engineers drew up plans for the tunnel, and in 1882 the British government began building the tunnel. However, because of fears that the tunnel would be used for invasion, it was left unfinished.

SHAPES OF TUNNELS

Tunnels are built in different shapes. The shape depends upon the function of the tunnel and the type of ground the tunnel is dug through. Tunnel shapes are listed below.

CIRCULAR
Round tunnels often used for going through soft ground or under water. They are most commonly used to carry water.

VERTICAL SIDEWALL
Round at the top and square at the bottom, this tunnel shape is used for roads.

HORSESHOE
Shaped like a horseshoe, this tunnel is used in soft ground when a flat floor is required.

BASKET HANDLE
A wide tunnel used for two or more roads. The shape is curved like a basket handle.

TYPES OF TUNNELS

DRIVEN
A tunnel drilled and blasted through rock, and usually through mountains. This type of tunnel is self-supporting.

SOFT GROUND
A tunnel dug through sand, clay, or wet ground. The walls are reinforced for support.

IMMERSED TUBE
A tunnel is dug, and a tube is immersed into the tunnel to give extra support under rivers or lakes.

CUT AND COVER
A trench is dug, the passageway is built, and the top is covered with earth.

A Calendar for Kids

365 DAYS TO CELEBRATE, DISCOVER, AND REMEMBER

The days of the year would be pretty dull if they were simply numbered from 1 to 365 without special holidays, birthdays, and events. This calendar was designed just for kids to celebrate the serious as well as the silly days of 1988. Make each day special by discovering a new fact, remembering an important person, or amusing yourself with an off-beat celebration.

Key to Symbols

★ **Holidays**   ◆ **Events**   ✳ **Birthdays**

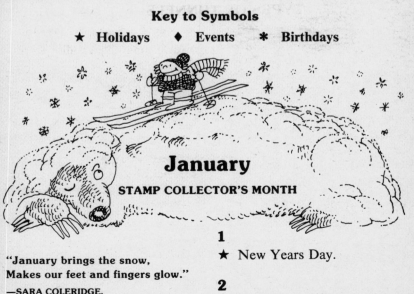

January

STAMP COLLECTOR'S MONTH

"January brings the snow,
Makes our feet and fingers glow."
—SARA COLERIDGE,
The Garden Year

1
★ New Years Day.

2
★ Good Luck Day.

3

♦ Sip-a-Drink-Through-a-Straw-Day. The wax drinking straw was patented in the U.S. on this day in 1888.

4

★ Trivia Day. This is the day to celebrate knowing all sorts of facts.

5

★ Twelfth Night. This day marked the end of medieval Christmas festivities. Time to take the Christmas tree down.

6

★ Feast of the Epiphany. The Christian holiday which celebrates the visit of the three kings to the baby Jesus, is observed on this day.

7

♦ In 1896, Fannie Farmer, famous American cookbook author, published her first cookbook.

8

✱ American singer Elvis Presley, born 1935.

9

♦ The first hot air balloon flight took place in the U.S., in 1793, at Philadelphia.

10

✱ Ethan Allen, Revolutionary War hero and leader of the Vermont soldiers known as the "Green Mountain Boys," born 1738.

11

♦ Banana Boat Day. Celebrate the invention of the plastic sundae dish used for the banana split sundae.

12

♦ The first American museum was organized on this day in Charleston, South Carolina, in 1773.

13

★ Stephen Foster Memorial Day. Remember the composer of 175 songs, among them "Oh, Susanna" and "My Old Kentucky Home."

14

✱ Albert Schweitzer, French medical missionary, born 1875. Dr. Schweitzer cared for native patients in his hospital in French Equatorial Africa. He was awarded the Nobel Peace Prize in 1956.

15

✱ Martin Luther King, Jr., American civil rights leader,

born 1929. His birthday is observed as a national holiday on January 19.

16

★ National Nothing Day. One day to not celebrate, observe, or honor anything.

17

✳ Benjamin Franklin, American inventor, statesman, and author (*Poor Richards Almanac*), born 1706.

18

✳ Celebrate the birthday of A.A. Milne, author of *Winnie the Pooh*, born 1882.

19

★ Confederate Heroes Day. Robert E. Lee, American Civil War general, was born on this day in 1807.

20

★ Hat Day. This is the day to celebrate the many kinds of hats worn by the people of the world.

21

★ National Clean Off Your Desk Day.

22

✳ English romantic poet Lord Byron (George Gordon) was born on this day in 1788.

23

✳ John Hancock, American patriot famous for his signature on the Declaration of Independence, was born on this day in 1737.

24

♦ In 1848, gold was discovered in California at Sutters Mill. This "gold rush" brought 40,000 prospectors to California in hopes of becoming rich.

25

✳ Robert Burns, Scottish poet ("Auld Lang Syne"), born 1759.

26

✳ American World War II hero, General Douglas MacArthur, born 1880. His famous quote was "I have come through, I shall return."

27

✳ Composer Wolfgang Amadeus Mozart was born on this day in Austria, 1756. He started playing the piano at age 3 and composing music at age 5.

28

* Swiss scientist and explorer twins, Auguste and Jean Piccard, born 1884. The Piccard brothers were known for their record-breaking balloon ascents into the stratosphere.

29

* Birthday of Thomas Paine, American Revolutionary War hero and author of the pamphlet "Common Sense," born 1737.

30

★ Swap-the-Brown-Bag-Lunch-Day. To liven up lunchtime, exchange lunch with a friend.

31

♦ The first successful U.S. satellite, *Explorer I*, was launched on this day in 1958.

February

BLACK HISTORY MONTH

"February brings the rain,
Thaws the frozen lake again."
—SARA COLERIDGE
The Garden Year

1

★ National Freedom Day.

2

★ Groundhog Day. According to legend, if the groundhog sees his shadow when he comes out on this day, there will be six more weeks of winter.

3

* Elizabeth Blackwell, first American woman doctor, born 1821.

4

* Charles Lindbergh, American aviator who made the first solo non-stop flight across the Atlantic Ocean, born 1902.

5

✳ Hank Aaron, baseball's "Home Run King," born 1934.

6

★ Midwinter Day. Winter is half over.

7

✳ Birthday of English novelist, Charles Dickens, born 1812. Dickens wrote some of the greatest novels of all time, such as *Oliver Twist* and *Great Expectations.*

8

♦ The Boy Scouts of America was established in the U.S., 1910. This organization was originally founded in England in 1908, by Sir Robert Baden-Powell.

9

♦ The U.S. National Weather Service was established on this day in 1870.

10

✳ Jimmy Durante, U.S. comedian famous for his nose, born 1893.

11

★ National Inventors Day. It's also the birthday of U.S. inventor Thomas Alva Edison, born 1847.

12

✳ Lincoln's Birthday. Abraham Lincoln, 16th U.S. president, born 1809.

13

♦ The first magazine in the U.S., *The American Magazine,* was published in 1741.

14

★ Valentine's Day.

15

✳ Susan B. Anthony Day. This American woman's rights pioneer was born in 1820.

16

♦ The first daily television news in the U.S. was broadcast on NBC in 1948.

17

♦ The National Congress of Parents and Teachers Association was established in the U.S., 1897. This association sponsors parent-teacher associations (PTAs) in schools across the United States.

18

♦ In 1930, astronomer Clyde Tombaugh confirmed the existence of the planet Pluto at Lowell Observatory in Flagstaff, Arizona.

19

* Polish astronomer Nicolaus Copernicus, born 1473. He was the first astronomer to determine that the planets revolved around the sun.

20

♦ In 1962, John Glenn became the first U.S. astronaut to orbit the earth.

21

♦ The first U.S. telephone book was issued to residents of New Haven, Connecticut, in 1878.

22

* Washington's Birthday. The first U.S. president, George Washington, was born on this day in 1732.

23

* Samuel Pepys, English diarist of London's Great Fire, born 1633.

24

* American artist of seascapes and landscapes, Winslow Homer, born 1836.

25

♦ The first U.S. savings bank opened in 1819.

26

* William F. Cody, American army scout and wild west showman (known as Buffalo Bill), born 1846.

27

* American consumer advocate Ralph Nader, born 1934.

28

* French writer Michael de Montaigne, the first to use the term "essay," born 1533.

29

★ Leap Year Day, every four years.

March

NATIONAL PEANUT MONTH

"March brings breezes, loud and
    shrill,
To stir the dancing daffodils."

—SARA COLERIDGE
The Garden Year

1

★ National Pig Day. This is the day to recognize pigs as one of most useful and intelligent domesticated animals.

2

✳ Dr. Seuss (Theodore Seuss Geisel), American author (*Green Eggs and Ham, The Butter Battle Book*), born 1904.

3

★ Dolls Festival, Japan. Hina Mutsuri, the Japanese doll festival, is celebrated by displaying favorite playthings.

4

♦ Celebrate the U.S. Constitution, declared in effect on this day in 1789.

5

✳ U.S. piano maker William Steinway born 1836.

6

✳ Michelangelo Buonarroti, Italian sculptor and painter, born 1475.

7

✳ U.S. botanist Luther Burbank, breeder of the white potato and more than 800 kinds of flowers, fruits, and vegetables, was born on this day in 1849.

8

✳ Joseph Lee, American developer of children's playgrounds, born 1862.

9

✳ Amerigo Vespucci, Italian explorer and navigator, for whom the Americas were named, born in 1451.

10

♦ Alexander Graham Bell made the first telephone call in 1876. He called his assistant and said: "Mr. Watson, come here, I want you".

11

♦ The anniversary of the death of John Chapman, known as Johnny Appleseed, 1847.

12

♦ The anniversary of the Great Blizzard of 1888 when 40 to 50 inches of snow with gale force winds covered the northeastern U.S.

13

♦ The planet Uranus was discovered in 1781 by German-English astronomer Sir William Herschel.

14

✱ Casey Jones (John Luther Jones), American railroad engineer hero, born 1864.

15

♦ Ides of March. This day commemorates the assassination of Roman emperor Julius Caesar in 44 B.C.

16

♦ First liquid-fuel-powered rocket was launched in 1926.

17

★ St. Patricks Day.

18

♦ On this day in 1965, Soviet cosmonaut Alexei Leonov became the first person to walk in space.

19

♦ Swallow's Day. Celebrate the yearly return of the swallows to Capistrano, California.

20

★ Celebrate Spring Day.

21

★ Memory Day. A day dedicated to improving memory skills.

22

★ National Goof-Off Day. Organized by people who believe in taking one day in the year to "goof off."

23

♦ Liberty Day. Celebrate the anniversary of American patriot Patrick Henry's famous speech ". . . give me liberty or give me death."

24

★ American Agriculture Day. This is a day to honor the dedication of American farmers.

25

♦ The first public demonstration of pancake-making occurred in a New York City restaurant window in 1882.

26

✳ Robert Frost, American poet ("Stopping by Woods on a Snowy Evening"), born 1874.

27

✳ Wilhelm Conrad Roentgen, German scientist and discoverer of x-rays, born 1845.

28

♦ Nathaniel Briggs of New Hampshire was granted a patent for a washing machine on this day in 1905.

29

★ Vietnam Veterans Day.

30

♦ The U.S. purchased Alaska from Russia in 1867.

31

✳ Robert Ross McBurney, founder of the American YMCA (Young Men's Christian Association), born 1837.

April

NATIONAL HUMOR MONTH

"Sweet April showers
Do spring May flowers."
—THOMAS TUSSER
April's Husbandry

1

★ April Fool's Day.

2

★ International Children's Book Day.

3

✳ Washington Irving, American writer ("The Legend of Sleepy Hollow"), born 1783.

4

* Linus Yale, American inventor of the cylinder lock, born 1821.

5

* Black educator and leader Booker T. Washington born 1856.

6

* Harry Houdini (Erich Weiss), American magician and escape artist, born 1874.

7

★ World Health Day.

8

♦ Spanish explorer Juan Ponce de Leon discovered Florida and planted orange trees there in 1513.

9

♦ The first American public library opened in Peterborough, New Hampshire, in 1833.

10

♦ Be Kind to Animals Day. The ASPCA (American Society for the Prevention of Cruelty to Animals) was established in 1866.

11

♦ On this day in 1947, Jackie Robinson joined the Brooklyn Dodgers as the first black major league baseball player.

12

♦ The strongest natural wind, 231 miles per hour, was recorded on this day in 1934 at Mount Washington, New Hampshire.

13

* U.S. President Thomas Jefferson, pictured on the U.S. nickel, was born in 1743.

14

♦ The first edition of Noah Webster's *American Dictionary of the English Language* was published in 1828.

15

★ National Griper's Day. If no one has listened to your complaints before, this is the day to complain and be heard.

16

* Charlie Chaplin, British-American film star, born 1889.

17

★ Verrazano Day. Italian explorer Giovanni da Verrazano discovered New York Harbor in 1524.

18

♦ In 1775, American Paul Revere made his famous midnight ride to warn the colonists of the British march on Concord, Massachusetts.

19

♦ In 1892, the first American-made automobile was driven and named the "buggyout" by its maker, Charles Duryea of Springfield, Massachusetts.

20

♦ On this day in 1534, the French explorer Jacques Cartier reached the island of Labrador. Labrador is the mainland area of Newfoundland, Canada.

21

♦ Birthday of Rome. Rome, Italy, was founded in 753 B.C.

22

★ Earth Day. This is a day to celebrate the earth and to think about ways to protect the environment.

23

✳ Serge Prokofiev, Russian composer (*Peter and the Wolf*), born 1891.

24

♦ The world's largest collection of stored knowledge is in the Library of Congress, established in Washington, D.C., in 1800.

25

♦ On this day in 1921, New York became the first state to require license plates on cars.

26

✳ John James Audubon, American naturalist, born 1875.
✳ Frederick Law Olmstead, American landscape architect (Central Park), born 1822.

27

✳ Samuel Morse, American inventor of the Morse Code, was born on this day in 1791.

28

♦ In 1789, history's most famous mutiny took place on board the HMS *Bounty.*

29

✳ American newspaper editor and publisher William Randolph Hearst was born on this day in 1863.

30

★ Walpurgis Night. In folklore, fairies welcome back the warm weather on this day.

May

BIKE SAFETY MONTH

"... the merry month of May..."
—RICHARD BARNFIELD
In Divers Humours

1

★ May Day. A day for May baskets, maypoles, and flower festivals.

2

✱ Henry Robert, American author of *Robert's Rules of Order*, born 1837. His book set behavior standards for business meetings.

3

◆ The first U.S. public, non-commercial radio network began programming in 1971.

4

◆ On this day in 1626, Dutch governor Peter Minuit bought Manhattan island for 24 dollars worth of merchandise.

5

★ Cinco de Mayo. This Mexican national holiday celebrates the Mexican victory over the French in the Battle of Puebla, 1867. Festivals take place in U.S. cities with large Mexican-American populations.

6

◆ On this day in 1954, British doctor and athlete Roger Bannister was the first to run a mile in under four minutes.

7

✱ Celebrate two birthdays today—German composer Johannes Brahms, born 1833, and Russian composer Peter Ilyich Tchaikovsky born 1840.

8

◆ Spanish explorer Hernando de Soto discovered the Mississippi River on this day in 1541.

9

✱ Sir James Barrie, Scottish author of *Peter Pan*, born 1860.

10

★ Mother's Day (1987; Mother's Day will be on the 8th in 1988). The first Mother's Day was celebrated in 1908 at the suggestion of Anna Jarvis of Philadelphia.

11

✻ Dancer and choreographer Martha Graham born 1894.

12

✻ English limerick writer Edward Lear, born 1812.

13

♦ In 1607, the first permanent English settlement was established in Jamestown, Virginia.

14

✻ Gabriel Fahrenheit, German-Dutch physicist who invented the mercury thermometer, born 1686.

15

★ Peace Officers' Memorial Day. A day to mark the memory of peace officers who have died in the line of duty.

16

♦ The first movie Oscars were awarded in 1929 by the Academy of Motion Picture Arts and Sciences.

17

♦ Celebrate the birthday of the New York Stock Exchange, founded on this day in 1792.

18

♦ In 1852, Massachusetts became the first state to make school attendance mandatory.

19

✻ Opera singer Nellie Melba (Helen Porter Mitchell), for whom the Peach Melba dessert was created, was born in 1861.

20

✻ Dolly (Dorothea) Madison, popular American First Lady, born 1768.

21

♦ American Red Cross founded by Clara Barton, 1881.

22

✻ Sir Arthur Conan Doyle, Scottish-English author and creator of fictional detective Sherlock Holmes, born 1859.

23

✻ German doctor, Friedrich Anton Mesmer, the first to use hypnotism to treat patients, born 1815.

24

♦ Celebrate the birthday of the Brooklyn Bridge. In 1883, the Brooklyn Bridge over the East River in New York City was opened.

25

★ National Missing Children's Day.

26

✳ Sally Ride, the first American woman to travel in space, born 1951.

27

★ Memorial Day. A day of prayer for permanent peace.

28

✳ Jim Thorpe, American football player and Olympic gold medalist, born 1888.

29

♦ Sir Edmund Hillary of New Zealand and Tenzing Norkay of Nepal became the first to reach the summit of Mt. Everest in 1953.

30

♦ The Hall of Fame of Great Americans opened at New York University, New York City, in 1901.

31

✳ Walt Whitman, American poet (*Leaves of Grass*), was born on this day in 1819.

June

DAIRY MONTH

"June is Busting Out All Over"
—OSCAR HAMMERSTEIN,
Carousel

1

★ Nathaniel Ulysses Turtle Day. Celebrate the new year of the turtle.

2

♦ The first night baseball game was played in Fort Wayne, Indiana, in 1883.

3

* Jefferson Davis Day. Confederate President Jefferson Davis, born 1808.

4

♦ On this day in A.D. 1070, in Roquefort, France, sheep's milk cheese with blue-green mold was discovered to be edible.

5

★ World Environment Day.

6

♦ The world's first drive-in movie theatre opened in Camden, New Jersey, in 1933.

7

♦ American frontiersman Daniel Boone began exploring Kentucky in 1769.

8

* American architect Frank Lloyd Wright born 1869.

9

★ Senior Citizen's Day.

10

* American physician John

Morgan, responsible for the first medical school in the American colonies, was born on this day in 1735.

11

* King Kamehameha I Day. The unifier of the Hawaiian Islands was born in 1758.

12

♦ The Baseball Hall of Fame was opened in Cooperstown, New York, on this day in 1939. Among its first members were Ty Cobb, Honus Wagner, Babe Ruth, Christy Mathewson, Walter Johnson, and Napoleon (Larry) Lajoie.

13

★ Alexander the Great Memorial Day (honors the ancient Macedonian king).

14

★ Flag Day.

15

★ Smile Power Day. Today is a reminder of the joy a smile brings.

16

♦ In 1963, Soviet cosmonaut Valentina Tereshkova became the first woman to travel into space.

17

♦ The term "G.I. Joe" first appeared in a comic strip in the magazine *Yank* in 1942.

18

★ International Picnic Day.

19

★ Father's Day (1988). The first observance of Father's Day took place in 1910 in Spokane, Washington.

20

♦ The Great Seal of the United States was adopted by Congress in 1782.

21

★ First day of summer.

22

★ National Fink Day. Finks from all over the world gather in Fink, Texas, for a reunion.

23

★ Midsummer's Eve, Europe's celebration of summer.

24

♦ On this day in 1947, "flying saucers" were first reported; they were spotted over Mount Ranier, Washington.

25

♦ The first TV show in color was broadcast by CBS in 1951.

26

♦ The world's first board-walk opened in Atlantic City, New Jersey, in 1870.

27

✱ Helen Keller, American author and advocate of help for the blind, born 1880.

28

♦ World War I began on this day in 1914 and ended on this same day in 1919 with the Treaty of Versailles.

29

★ The feast days for St. Peter, patron saint of fishermen and sailors, and St. Paul, patron saint of tentmakers and rope-makers, are celebrated on this day.

30

♦ On this day in 1859, a French acrobat and aerialist, Charles Blondin, walked across Niagara Falls on a tightrope.

July

NATIONAL HOT DOG MONTH

"Hot July brings cooling showers,
Apricots and gilly-flowers."

—SARA COLERIDGE,
The Garden Year

1

♦ The first U.S. postage stamps were issued, 1847.

2

★ Halfway Day. The year is half over at noon, Standard Time.

3

♦ Dog Days. The six hottest weeks of summer in the Northern Hemisphere begin today.

4

★ Happy Birthday U.S.A. The United States of America was born in 1776.

5

✽ American circus showman P.T. Barnum was born in 1810.

6

✽ Beatrix Potter, author and illustrator (*Peter Rabbit*), born in London, England, 1866.

7

✽ Marc Chagall, Russian-French painter and graphic artist, born 1887.

8

♦ The first U.S. passport was issued to Francis Barre in 1796.

9

✽ Elias Howe, the U.S. inventor of the sewing machine, born 1819.

10

✽ On this day in 1839, American painter James Abbott McNeill Whistler was born. Whistler's most famous portrait is titled "Arrangement in Grey and Black, No. 1: The Artist's Mother," popularly referred to as "Whistler's Mother."

11

★ National Cheer-Up-the-Lonely Day.

12

✳ Buckminister Fuller, American engineer and designer of the geodesic dome, was born in 1895.

13

★ Night Walk Day. The eve of Bastille Day is celebrated in France by torchlight parades.

14

★ Bastille Day. Today is Independence Day in France. It commemorates the capture of the Bastille (a tower used as a prison) and the start of the French revolution.

15

★ National Ice Cream Day.

16

◆ The first world atlas, or book of maps, was printed on this day in 1482. The maps had been drawn by Claudius Ptolemy in A.D. 150.

17

✳ American detective writer Stanley Erle Gardner, born 1889. He is best known for his Perry Mason stories.

18

✳ Dick Button, American Olympic gold medalist in figure skating, was born in 1929.

19

◆ The first U.S. Women's Rights Convention was held in Seneca Falls, New York, 1920.

20

◆ The first people to land on the moon were American astronauts Neil Armstrong and Edwin "Buzz" Aldrin, Jr., in 1969.

21

◆ A legendary train robbery in U.S. history, masterminded by outlaw Jesse James, took place on this day in 1873.

22

◆ According to legend, on this day in 1376 the piper who wasn't paid for piping rats out of Hamelin, Germany, piped the children out of town.

23

◆ The ice cream cone was invented at the St. Louis World's Fair in 1904.

24

✳ American aviator Amelia Earhart, the first woman to fly solo across the Atlantic Ocean, born 1898.

25

* Louise Brown of Oldham, England, the first baby conceived in a test tube, was born in 1978.

26

♦ The first textbook about the International Language, Esperanto, was published on this day in 1887.

27

♦ The first Atlantic cable between Newfoundland and Ireland, covering 1,686 miles, was laid on this day in 1866.

28

♦ In 1933, the first singing telegram was delivered to singer Rudy Vallee on his birthday.

29

♦ Today is the anniversary of the first transcontinental telephone conversation in the U.S. (in 1914).

30

* Henry Ford, American auto manufacturer and assembly line developer, born 1863.

31

♦ The first U.S. patent ever issued was granted to Samuel Hopkins in 1790 for processing a potash substance used to make soap and glass.

August

SANDWICH MONTH

"August brings the sheaves of corn, Then the harvest home is borne."

—SARA COLERIDGE, *The Garden Year*

1

* Francis Scott Key, American author of the National Anthem, born 1799.

2

* French architect, Pierre Charles L'Enfant, who designed the plan for the city of Washington, D.C., was born on this day in 1754.

3

♦ On this day in 1492, Christopher Columbus, with 3 ships and a crew of 90 men, set sail for China, but reached the Americas instead.

4

♦ Coast Guard Day. The U.S. Coast Guard was founded on this day in 1790.

5

★ Family Day.

6

★ Summer is Half Over Day.

7

♦ In 1888, Theophilus Von Kannel of Philadelphia patented the revolving door.

8

♦ The U.S. Congress adopted the dollar as a unit of money for the national currency on this day in 1786.

9

♦ In 1936, Jesse Owens, a track runner and jumper from the U.S., won his fourth gold medal at the summer Olympics in Berlin, Germany.

10

♦ On this day in 1625, work began on the world's first astronomical observatory in Greenwich, England, from which the world's time is regulated.

11

* Christiann Eijkman, Dutch discover of Vitamin B and Nobel Prize winner in Medicine, born 1858.

12

* Abbott Thayer, American painter and creator of the concept of camouflage (known as Thayer's Law), was born on this day in 1849.

13

★ International Left-Handers Day. All left-handed people get special attention and recognition today.

14

♦ The *Book of Psalms,* the first printed book, was published in 1457.

15

★ National Failures Day. Have the courage to try despite the chance of failure.

16

♦ Gold was discovered in the Klondike region of Alaska in 1896.

17

✱ Davy Crockett, American frontiersman and soldier, was born in 1786.

18

✱ The first American child of English parents was born on this day in 1587. Her name was Virginia Dare.

19

★ National Aviation Day.

20

♦ In 1964, U.S. President Lyndon Johnson signed the anti-poverty bill.

21

✱ Ozma's Birthday. The Queen of Oz, from the *Oz* books, was born on this day.

22

♦ The famous Lincoln-Douglas debates between presidential candidates Stephen Douglas and Abraham Lincoln took place in 1858.

23

✱ American poet Edgar Lee Masters, author of *The Spoon River Anthology,* was born on this day in 1869.

24

♦ American Cornelius Swartout patented the waffle iron in 1869.

25

✱ Allan Pinkerton, American detective and founder of Pinkerton Security company, was born in Scotland in 1819.

26

♦ In 1883, Krakatoa, a volcano on the Indonesian volcanic island of the same name, erupted. It was the biggest volcanic eruption in history, heard 3,000 miles away.

27

♦ Oil, a fossil fuel, was first drilled in the U.S. on this day in 1859.

28

✱ Elizabeth Seton, the first American-born saint, was born in New York City in 1774.

29

♦ Chop Suey, an American-style Chinese dish, was prepared and served for the first time in New York City by the Chef of Li Hung Chang in 1896.

30

✱ Mary Wollstonecraft Shelley, wife of the poet Shelley and author of *Frankenstein*, was born in England in 1797.

31

✱ Maria Montessori, Italian educator and originator of the Montessori method of education, born 1870.

September

READ A NEW BOOK MONTH

"Up from the meadows rich with
    corn,
Clear in the cool September morn."

—JOHN GREENLEAF WHITTIER,
Barbara Frietchie

1

✱ American author Edgar Rice Burroughs, who wrote 24 *Tarzan* books, was born on this day in 1875.

2

♦ In 1789, the United States established the Treasury Department.

3

♦ In 1976, the U.S. satellite *Viking I* landed on Mars and sent photos of the Martian landscape back to Earth.

4

♦ Newspaper Carrier Day. Today is the anniversary of the hiring of 10-year-old Chicagoan, Barney Flaherty, the first "newsboy" in the U.S.

5

★ National Be Late for Something Day.

6

✱ Jane Addams, American social worker and Nobel Peace Prize winner, born 1860.

7

✱ Today is the birthday of Grandma Moses (Anna Mary Robertson Moses), who started painting at the age of 78. She was born in New York in 1860.

8

* British actor Peter Sellers, who portrayed Inspector Clouseau in the *Pink Panther* movies, born 1925.

9

♦ The American Bowling Congress was organized on this day in 1895.

10

★ Swap Ideas Day.

11

♦ In 1962, the British rock group, the Beatles, made their first recordings, "Love Me Do" and "P.S., I Love You."

12

★ Snack-A-Pickle Day.

13

♦ In 1609, Henry Hudson sailed up the Hudson River to Albany and claimed the area for the Dutch.

14

♦ In 1752, the American colonies and Great Britain decided to use the Gregorian calendar to mark time. The Gregorian calendar changed New Year's Day from March 25 to January 1.

15

★ World Peace Day.

16

♦ On this day in 1620, the *Mayflower* set sail from Plymouth, England. Sixty-six days later, it arrived in Plymouth, Massachusetts.

17

★ Citizenship Day.

18

♦ In 1917, the Honolulu Ad Club patented the ukelele.

19

♦ In 1928, Mickey Mouse appeared in his first movie, *Steamboat Willie.*

20

♦ Portuguese explorer Ferdinand Magellan, sailing under the Spanish flag, began the first voyage around the world in 1519.

21

♦ The U.S. Post Office was established on this day in 1789.

22

★ National Good Neighbor Day.

23

♦ First day of Autumn.
* Birthday of American singer, Bruce Springsteen, born in 1949.

24

∗ Jim Henson, U.S. puppeteer and creator of the Muppets, was born in 1936.

25

♦ Spanish explorer Vasco de Balboa discovered and named the Pacific Ocean in 1513.

26

∗ Johnny Appleseed (John Chapman), American apple tree planter, born 1774.

27

∗ Thomas Nast, the American political cartoonist who created cartoon symbols for the Democratic (donkey) and Republican (elephant) political parties, was born in 1840.

28

★ Confucius Day. The birthday of Chinese philosopher, Confucius (K'ung Fu-Tzu), is celebrated as a national holiday in Taiwan. He was born in 551 B.C. and died at the age of 72, having been a teacher for 40 years.

29

∗ Gene Autry, the singing cowboy who starred in over 80 western films, was born on this day in 1907.

30

★ Ask a Stupid Question Day. On this day, curious people are encouraged to ask questions, no matter how silly they may seem.

October

NATIONAL POPCORN MONTH

"Fresh October brings the pheasant;
Then to gather nuts is pleasant."

—SARA COLERIDGE,
The Garden Year

1

♦ In 1847, American astronomer Maria Mitchell discovered a new comet and was awarded a gold medal from the King of Denmark.

2

♦ The first "Peanuts" comic strip, by Charles Schulz, was published on this day in 1950.

3

✱ British parasitologist Sir Patrick Manson, whose research led to the discovery that mosquitoes are carriers of the disease, malaria, was born in 1844.

4

★ Today is the feast day of St. Francis of Assisi, the patron saint of animals.

5

♦ In 1921, the World Series of baseball was broadcast on the radio for the first time. The New York Giants beat the New York Yankees, five games to three.

6

♦ The first major chess tournament was held in New York City on this day in 1857.

7

✱ James Whitcomb Riley, American author ("Little Orphan Annie"), born 1849.

8

♦ According to legend, Mrs. O'Leary's cow kicked over a lantern in a barn, starting the great Chicago fire disaster in 1871.

9

♦ Leif Ericson, Norse explorer, landed in North America in A.D. 1000

10

♦ The tuxedo, a dress suit for men, was first worn in the U.S. on this day in 1886.

11

★ Pulaski Memorial Day. This is the day to remember the Polish-born Revolutionary War hero, Casimir Pulaski.

12

★ Columbus Day. Christopher Columbus arrived in the New World on this day in 1492.

13

♦ The U.S. Navy was established in 1775.

14

♦ In 1947, U.S. Air Force Captain Charles (Chuck) Yeager became the first to travel faster than the speed of sound.

15

★ National Grouch Day. All grouches are recognized today.

16

★ World Food Day. This is the day to make people aware of the worldwide struggle against hunger.

17

★ Black Poetry Day. Today, the contributions of black poets to American life are recognized.

18

✱ Actor George C. Scott, born 1927.

19

♦ The Revolutionary War ended at the Battle of Yorktown in 1781.

20

♦ The Ringling Brothers and Barnum and Bailey Circus ("The Greatest Show on Earth") opened in New York City in 1873.

21

♦ Thomas Edison invented the electric incandescent lamp in 1879.

22

✱ Annette Funicello, U.S. actress and an original Disney Mouseketeer, was born in 1942.

23

✱ Nicolas Appert, French chef and chemist who devised a system of canning foods, was born on this day in 1752.

24

★ United Nations Day.

25

✱ Spanish painter, sculptor, and engraver Pablo Picasso was born in 1881.

26

♦ Spanish jacks (donkeys), which were bred with horses to produce mules, were first imported to the U.S. on this day.

27

✱ President Theodore (Teddy) Roosevelt was born on this day in 1858. A cartoon showing how he once saved a bear cub inspired the popular stuffed toy, the teddy bear.

28

♦ The Statue of Liberty was dedicated on this day in 1886.

29

✱ American gospel singer Mahalia Jackson was born in 1911.

30

♦ The *War of the Worlds*, a 1938 radio drama describing a Martian invasion of New Jersey, was mistaken by many people for an actual news bulletin.

31

★ Halloween.

November

NATIONAL ICE SKATING MONTH

"Dull November brings the blast;
Then the leaves are whirling fast."
—SARA COLERIDGE,
The Garden Year

1

★ All Saints Day. This is the day to honor those saints who have no special feast day.

2

✻ American pioneer and explorer, Daniel Boone, born 1734.

3

✻ John Montague, Earl of Sandwich and supposed creator of the sandwich, was born on this day in 1718.

4

✻ Will Rogers, American humorist and humanitarian, born 1879.

5

★ Guy Fawkes Day. The "Gunpowder Plot" of 1605 is celebrated in Canada and England with fireworks and parties. This conspiracy to blow up the English parliament and King James I by English Catholics was led by Guy Fawkes.

6

✻ John Philip Sousa, American band conductor and composer of marches, born 1854.

7

✱ Marie Curie, Polish-English chemist and physicist, co-discoverer with her husband, Pierre, of radium, born 1867.

8

✱ English astronomer, Edmund Halley, the first to predict the return of a comet, was born in 1656.

9

◆ East Coast Blackout Anniversary. A massive electric power failure, darkening the northeastern U.S. and Ontario, occurred on this day in 1965.

10

✱ Vachel Lindsay, American poet who roamed America for 20 years giving poems away, was born on this day in 1879.

11

★ Veterans Day.

12

✱ Rumanian gymnast Nadia Comaneci, winner of 3 Olympic gold medals, was born on this day in 1961.

13

✱ Scottish poet and novelist, Robert Louis Stevenson, was born in 1850. *Treasure Island* is one of his novels.

14

◆ On this day in 1889, journalist Nellie Bly (Elizabeth Cochrane) embarked on a trip that took her around the world (without cars or planes) in less than 80 days.

15

★ Children's Shrine Visiting Day. In Japan, on this day, children are taken to shrines to offer thanks for good health and fortune.

16

✱ W.C. Handy, American composer and bandleader, was born in 1873. He is known as the "Father of the Blues."

17

★ Homemade Bread Day. Enjoy the making and eating of homemade bread.

18

✱ George Gallup, famous U.S. public opinion pollster, born 1901.

19

◆ Gettysburg Address Day. President Abraham Lincoln made his famous Gettysburg Address on this day in 1863.

20

✱ Peregrine White's Birth-

day. On this day in 1620, the first child born in the New England colonies to English parents was Peregrine White.

21

★ World Hello Day. Guten Tag (German), Bon Giorno (Italian), Bon Jour (French), and Buenos Dias (Spanish) all mean Hello.

22

♦ The National Hockey league was established in Montreal, Canada, in 1917.

23

✳ Horror Movie Day. Horror Movie Actor Boris Karloff, who played Frankenstein and the Mummy, was born in 1887.

24

★ Thanksgiving Day (1988).

25

✳ American industrialist and philanthropist, Andrew Carnegie, born 1835.

26

♦ Sojourner Truth Memorial Day. This is the day to honor American black abolitionists.

27

✳ Buffalo Bob (Bob Smith), star of the popular kids' TV show, "Howdy Doody," was born in 1917.

28

♦ The first skywriting in America was seen over New York City on this day in 1922.

29

✳ Louisa May Alcott, author of *Little Women*, born 1832.

30

✳ Mark Twain (Samuel Clemens), American author of *Tom Sawyer* and *Huckleberry Finn*, was born in 1835.

PSSST!

December

GOOD NEIGHBOR MONTH

"Chill December brings the sleet,
Blazing fire, and Christmas treat."

—SARA COLERIDGE,
The Garden Year

1

♦ The U.S. civil rights movement began in Montgomery, Alabama, in 1955 when Rosa Parks refused to give up her bus seat to a white rider.

2

★ Pan American Health Day.

3

✳ Sir Rowland Hill, who introduced the first adhesive postage stamps, was born in England in 1795.

4

✳ Luther Hasey Gulick, American co-founder of the Campfire Girls of America, was born in 1865.

5

✳ Walt Disney, American producer, animator, and creator of Disneyland and Disney World, was born in 1901.

6

★ Feast of St. Nicholas. In some European countries, it is believed that St. Nicholas brings gifts to children on this day.

7

♦ Pearl Harbor Day. The U.S. entered World War II on this day in 1941, when Pearl Harbor, Hawaii, was attacked by the Japanese.

8

✳ Eli Whitney, American inventor of the cotton gin, born 1765.

9

✳ Clarence Birdseye, Amer-

ican inventor of frozen foods, was born on this day in 1886.

10

★ Human Rights Day.

11

* Annie Jump Cannon, American astronomer and discoverer of five stars, was born in 1863.

12

★ National Ding-A-Ling Day. This is the day to promote the idea that a ding-a-ling is a wonderful person.

13

★ St. Lucia Day. In Sweden, children serve their parents breakfast in bed in honor of this day, which celebrates the return of light after the darkest time of year.

14

* French doctor Nostradamus, famous for his predictions of the future, was born Michel de Notredame in 1503.

15

★ Bill of Rights Day. Celebrate Americans' freedom of speech, religion, press, and assembly.

16

* Ludwig von Beethoven, German composer of nine symphonies and other works, some while he was totally deaf, born 1770.

17

♦ In 1903, Americans Orville and Wilbur Wright made the first successful airplane flight. Orville won the toss of a coin and was the first to fly in their biplane, "Flyer."

18

* Joseph Grimalde, one of the greatest clowns in history, was born in England in 1778.

19

♦ Christmas Greetings from Space Anniversary. In 1958, the U.S. satellite *Atlas* broadcast the first radio voice from space—a Christmas greeting from President Eisenhower.

20

♦ The Louisiana Purchase took place on this day in 1803, when the U.S. bought over a million square miles of land from the French.

21

★ Look at the Bright Side Day. Although winter begins on this day in the Northern Hemisphere, summer is being enjoyed in the Southern Hemisphere.

22

★ International Arbor Day. This is the day to promote the planting and preserving of trees around the world.

23

★ Feast of the Radishes. In Oaxaca, Mexico, small figures of people and animals carved out of radishes are sold at this festival.

24

★ Christmas Eve.

25

★ Christmas Day.

26

★ Boxing Day. In Great Britain, gifts are given to public ser-vants as thanks for their year-long services. The name comes from the Christmas boxes in which the gifts are put.

27

✱ English inventor and scientist, George Cayley, pilot of the world's first manned glider flight, was born in 1773.

28

♦ American William Semple patented chewing gum on this day in 1869.

29

✱ Charles MacIntosh, Scottish chemist who first bonded rubber to fabric to make raincoats, was born in 1776.

30

✱ Rudyard Kipling, English novelist known for his stories about India, was born in India in 1865.

31

★ New Years Eve.

Collections

People are collectors. All over the world, kids and adults are collecting just as they have for thousands of years. Coin collecting may have originally been the hobby of ancient kings, but today, people collect everything from coins to barn doors, from doorknobs to shoelaces.

People form clubs, hold conventions, and travel great distances to see collections displayed in museums and libraries. This chapter is all about collections and collectors.

What Kids Collect

It would be impossible to list all the things kids the world over are collecting today. What follows is a list of some of the most popular collector items among kids in the U.S.

Advertising items	Beads	Buckles
Animal figures	Bells	Buttons
Autographs	Bookmarks	Calendars
Badges	Books	Cans
Balls	Bottle caps	Cards (novelty, sports)

Cartoon strips
Cereal box prices
Checker sets
Chess sets
Chinese cookie fortunes
Combs
Comic books
Cowboy gear
Dolls and dollhouses
Erasers
Flags
Games
Greeting cards
Gum wrappers
Hats
Headbands
Hometown mementos

Jewelry
Keys
Key chains
Locks
Magazines
Maps
Marbles
Matchbook covers
Medals
Menus
Miniatures
Models
Paper dolls
Pennants
Pens
Pencils
Playing cards

Postcards
Posters
Programs
Puppets
Recipes
Records and tapes
Ribbons
Souvenirs
Stamps
Stickers
Teddy bears
Tee shirts
Toy banks
Trophies
Valentines
Unicorn figurines
Yo-yos

NATURE COLLECTIONS

Birds' nests
Birds' feathers
Butterflies

Flowers (dried)
Insects
Leaves
Mosses

Seashells
Sand
Rocks

A Collection of Collectors

MARTHA BEAULIEU
Wishbones

For 57 years, Martha Beaulieu of Holyoke, Massachusetts, has collected wishbones and hung them on pegs on the walls of her kitchen and pantry. Martha started her unusual collection when she was 32 years old and Franklin D. Roosevelt was president. The U.S. was recovering

from the Great Depression of the 1930s, and her family was lucky enough to have chicken for dinner every Sunday. Martha began to collect the wishbones as mementos. She kept on collecting. The most recent count of her wishbones totals 493 chicken, 201 turkey, 43 duck, 37 pheasant, and four partridge bones, for a grand total of 778 wishbones.

PETER BULL
Teddy Bears

Peter Bull's collection of teddy bears is the most famous in the world. His bears frequently make personal appearances and have been featured in movies and on television.

Mr. Bull, a British actor, was a great lover of bears. Most of his 350 teddy bears were given to him as gifts. He also collected bear items, such as bear-shaped clocks and bears depicted on clothing and dishes. Before he died in 1984, Mr. Bull made arrangements for his collection. Two of his bears were sent to live with special friends. The rest of the bears and bear items were given to the Toy & Model Museum in London, England.

JERRY DE FUCCIO
Comic Books

The son of a doctor, Jerry De Fuccio often went with his father on house calls. While he waited in the car, friendly neighbors gave him ice cream and comic books to read. He loved the comic books and began to collect them, but he had to hide them in his grandmother's house because his father disapproved of them. Today, his collection of 600 comic books, mostly saved from childhood, is a joy to him as well as a valuable investment. For example, he owns the first comic book to feature Superman, Action Comics #1, published in 1939.

MALCOLM FORBES
Toy Boats and Toy Soldiers

World-famous financier and publisher, Malcolm Forbes, is an avid collector. When Malcolm was eight years old, he began collecting comic books. At 15, he switched from comic books to Napoleon III memorabilia, and in his adult years, he began collecting toy boats and toy soldiers. The memory of the many hours spent playing with them and the loss of those childhood toys sparked an interest in collecting them. Today, his collection totals 80,000 toy soldiers and 500 toy boats. They are on permanent display in his museum located in the Forbes Building in New York City.

Malcolm Forbes grew up in a family of collectors and his own children are collectors as well. In fact, the Forbes family collections are so vast they are housed in four private museums in England, France, Morocco, and the United States. The Forbes family has been described as "America's First Family of Collectors."

MARGARET WOODBURY STRONG
Dollhouses and Dolls

Margaret Strong was born in 1897, the only child of a wealthy family in Rochester, New York. When she was very young, her mother gave her a dollhouse. It became her favorite toy. Soon she began to collect dollhouses and the dolls to go with them. She collected dolls from all over the world when she traveled with her parents. After a lifetime of collecting, Margaret Strong had accumulated 27,000 dolls—the world's largest private collection. When she died in 1969, her will provided that a museum be built to house her collection of dolls, dollhouses, and other toys. Her collection is now in the Strong Museum in Rochester, New York.

ELIZABETH TASHJIAN
Nuts

Elizabeth Tashjian admits that she is "nuts" about nuts and that she lives in a kind of "nuthouse." Ms. Tashjian is a nut collector. In fact, she has devoted the past 30 years of her life to collecting nuts, learning about nuts, painting nuts, and composing "nut" music. Her home in Old Lyme, Connecticut, is also the Nut Museum. Nuts are featured in the furniture, carpets, and paintings in the house. Her collection includes toy furniture and jewelry made from nuts. She has nuts from all over the world, including the world's largest nut—a 35-pound double coconut from the Seychelles Islands.

E. WHARTON-TIGAR
Trading Cards

Next to E. Wharton-Tigar's home in London, England, is another house. He bought the second house to hold his trading and tobacco cards. He has about a million such cards, the world's largest private collection. E. Wharton-Tigar began collecting in 1917 at the age of five; his first card was from the British Bird collection. His father wanted him to collect cigarette trading cards, so the youngster collected those his father brought back from business trips. Today, E. Wharton-Tigar is an international businessman and collects cards in every country of the world. He also writes to other collectors, advising them on collecting, cataloging, and displaying trading cards.

Collections To Visit

A "collector's paradise," perhaps the ultimate collection of collections, is the Smithsonian Institution in Washington, D.C. Within its 12 museums, there are more than 100 million objects on view. This vast collection includes 77 spacecrafts, 12 million postage stamps, 35,594 skeletons, 30,834 costumes, 6,214 African masks, and 4,500 meteorites. Other collections in the U.S., from the simple to the world-renowned, are listed below.

AUTOGRAPHS
New York Public Library
5th Avenue and 42nd Street
New York, New York 10018
One of the world's largest collections of autographs is housed in this library. The signatures of famous people such as Thomas Edison and Albert Einstein can be seen here. The special pride of this collection is the four complete sets of the signatures of those who signed the Declaration of Independence.

AUTOMOBILES
William F. Harrah Automobile
**   Museum**
401 Dermody Way
Sparks, Nevada 89431
The history of automobiles can be seen in this outstanding collection. On view are antique cars, classic cars, racing cars, and cars

that introduced innovations such as electric windows and tilted steering wheels.

BARBED WIRE
Barbed Wire Museum
614 Main Street
LaCrosse, Kansas 67548
Over 500 pieces of barbed wire are displayed in this one-of-a-kind collection. Since 1881, when barbed wire was invented, over a thousand different kinds of barbed wire have been made. Some of the types of barbed wire included in this collection are entanglement wire used for war, fencing pieces from foreign countries, and signal wire used in corn planters. But the highlight of the collection is a barbed-wire nest made by crows. It was taken from a tree in Kansas. The crows' nest weighs 72 pounds. It is believed that the crows made the nest of barbed wire because of the scarcity of other nest material in the area.

BOY SCOUT ITEMS
Boy Scout Museum
Murray State University
Murray, Kentucky 42071
Visitors to this museum can see over 30,000 items honoring Boy Scouts, including badges and uniforms dating back to 1910. Boy Scouts were a frequent subject for artist Norman Rockwell, and 54 of these works are in this collection. The museum also highlights the compass, an important tool for all Scouts. There are compasses here that date from the 15th century to the present time.

BUTTONS
Cooper-Hewitt Museum
2 East 91st Street
New York, New York 10028
Over 1,000 buttons from all over the world are on view here. There are buttons of every size and shape, made from animal horns, ivory, precious stones, wood, glass, and metal.

CHILDREN'S BOOKS
Pierpont Morgan Library
29 East 36th Street
New York, New York 10016
Among the treasures of this library is a large collection of children's books. It is one of the most comprehensive collections of its kind in the world. There are 225 outstanding books written and illustrated for children. For example, there is the original manuscript of Perrault's *Fairy Tales,* which features the first drawings of Little Red Riding Hood. There is also a first edition of *The Wizard of Oz.* This collection also boasts a large selection of schoolbooks, some of which are hundreds of years old.

CARTOON ART
**Museum of Cartoon Art
Comly Avenue
Port Chester, New York 10573**
Cartoon characters, like Mickey Mouse and Charlie Brown, decorate the carpets, ceilings, and washrooms of this museum. The collection itself is the largest collection of cartoon art in the world: 60,000 pieces of art are on display in this museum.

COWBOY MEMORABILIA
**National Cowboy Hall of Fame
and Western Heritage
Center
1700 Northeast 63rd Street
Oklahoma City, Oklahoma
73111**
Spurs, guns, hats, saddles, boots, and other cowboy gear have been collected in this museum, which honors the American cowboy. There are also life-size exhibits that portray the cowboy in authentic western settings.

DOLLHOUSES
**Washington Dolls' Houses and
Toy Museum
5236 44th Street, N.W.
Washington, D.C. 20015**
This extraordinary collection of dollhouses is on display in a miniature town. Small shops, stables, and schoolrooms are set among the houses. Hundreds of dolls in their original clothing as well as miniature furnishings fill the buildings. Most of the houses are Victorian. Other replicas include a turn-of-the-century quintet of Baltimore row houses and a 1903 New Jersey seaside hotel.

GAMES
**The Game Preserve
110 Spring Road
Peterborough, New Hampshire
03458**
A Parcheesi game from India, an English cribbage set, and a colonial American game of skittles are among this collection of games. There are over 1,000 old board and card games to view. Old-time ping-pong racquets and early pinball games complete this fascinating collection.

MARBLES
**Corning Museum of Glass
1 Museum Way
Corning, New York 14830**
Marbles of glass and stone, many of which are dented and dinged from use, make up this collection. Some of the 200 marbles are over a century old, and most were made in Germany. There are many candy-striped marbles in this collection, as well as sulfide marbles—clear marbles with white ceramic animals in-

side. A favorite of kids is a blue-and-white marble with a comic-strip character affixed to its surface. A written request must be made to see this collection which is not on public display.

MENUS
**New York Public Library
Room 121
5th Avenue and 42nd Street
New York, New York 10018**
Breakfast in the dining car of the Pennsylvania Railroad cost one dollar and included eight courses in 1882. A dinner of lamb chops served at a fancy New York restaurant in 1898 cost 60 cents. These are only two of the 25,000 menus in this collection. There are menus from hotels and steamships, as well as menus for special occasions, such as a state dinner hosted by President and Mrs. Rutherford B. Hayes. The oldest menus are from the 1840s, and the newest ones are from the 1920s.

PLAYING CARDS
**Playing Card Museum
The U.S. Playing Card
   Company
Beech and Park
Cincinnati, Ohio 45212**
This is the largest collection of antique playing cards in the world. It is so large that only parts of it can be displayed at one time. Among the many thou-

sands of decks are those designed by famous artists, like David, who designed decks for Napoleon. In the educational category, there are three decks that were used to instruct the French king, Louis XIV. There are cards that teach "signing," foreign languages, and bird-watching. Other categories of cards included in this collection are history, famous people, music, astronomy, theater, geography, and the Bible.

TRAINS
**The B&O Railroad Museum
Mt. Clare Station
Pratt and Poppleton Streets
Baltimore, Maryland 21223**
This is the largest railroad museum in the U.S. In its century-old roundhouse are 22 of the oldest and most historic locomotives and railroad cars in this collection. Altogether, the museum has 50 locomotives and many more passenger cars. The exhibit includes a huge model train set. The tracks for it took two years to build and carry 14 different steam and diesel trains.

In addition to the trains, there are other railroad items on display such as an 1841 copper water dispenser from which water was sold for one cent a glass.

The Language of Collectors

Many words have been coined by people who are avid collectors. The ten words below describe the interests of collectors and refer to the objects they collect.

Archtophile—A lover of teddy bears.

Bibliophile—A lover of books.

Circusiana—Items collected by circus lovers.

Decalomania—An interest in stickers and labels.

Deltiologist—A collector of picture postcards.

Erinnophilist—A collector of commemorative labels.

Numismatist—A collector of coins, tokens, or paper money.

Philatelist—A stamp collector.

Rabdophilist—A collector of walking sticks.

Railroadiana—Items collected by railroad lovers.

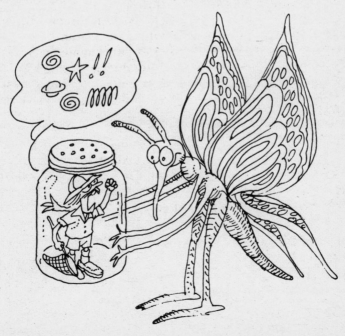

Computers and Robots

This is a quick reference guide for kids growing up in the "Age of the Computer." There is information about computer parts and an explanation of computer jargon, plus answers to kids' questions about computers. For those fascinated by robots, there is a section featuring robots of fact and fiction. You'll probably find yourself going back again to this handy guide to computers and robots.

Computers

A GUIDE TO COMPUTER PARTS

Cartridge—A plastic case with a ROM (read-only-memory) chip in it. The ROM chip may contain a game program or a computer language program. The cartridge fits into an opening in a computer.

Chip—A tiny computer part made of silicon (sand) which contains thousands of electrical pathways. The chips do the computer work; different chips do different jobs.

Disk—A round, flat plastic "record" encased in a square cardboard holder. The disk is used to store a program. Thin flexible disks are called floppy disks.

Disk Drive—A "player" much like a record turntable that runs the disk. It can read information from a disk or write new information onto a disk.

Hardware—All the parts of a computer including the keyboard, the monitor, and the inner parts.

Joystick—A box with a lever attached to a computer port. Moving the lever sends signals to the computer. A joystick may be used to play games or draw pictures on the computer screen.

Keyboard—The part of a computer with keys like a typewriter. Each time a key is pressed, a signal is sent to the computer.

Microprocessor—A computer chip that controls the computer. Also called the CPU (Central Processing Unit).

Monitor—The computer terminal screen.

Mouse—A small machine connected to a computer by a cable. It has buttons which can be pressed to make the computer do different things such as trace over graphs.

Port—A place in a computer where a monitor or other hardware can be connected.

Printer—A machine that prints a computer's output onto paper.

Software—Computer programs. Cartridges and disks are also called software.

"COMPUTERESE"

Address—The location in the computer where a piece of information is stored. Each address has its own number. The number helps the computer quickly find the information in its memory.

Boot—To start a computer. Most computers boot when the power is turned on.

Break—To stop a program on a computer when it is running.

Bug—An error in a program designed for a computer.

Crash—When the computer suddenly stops working.

Cursor—A moving symbol on a computer screen that indicates where the computer will write.

Debug—To find and fix an error in a computer program.

Hacker—A person who spends a great deal of time at a computer, learning how the computer works.

Load—To put a program into a computer.

Loop—A set of instructions a computer repeats a certain number of times.

Menu—The list of choices a program gives a computer user. The menu is shown on the screen of the computer.

Pixels—A series of dots which light up for a computer graphic.

Read—To get information from a cassette cartridge or disk through the computer.

Write—To put information from the computer onto a cassette or disk.

ANSWERS TO KIDS' QUESTIONS ABOUT COMPUTERS

What is a computer?

A computer is a machine that processes information according to a set of instructions called a program. Computers are capable of storing and retrieving information. A computer's ability to do this distinguishes it from other mathematical devices, such as the abacus and the electronic calculator.

Who invented the computer?

In general, the invention of the computer is rooted in the development of other mathematical machines, beginning with the ancient abacus. Vannevar Bush (1890-1974), an American engineer, was the first to build a machine called a computer in the present meaning of the word. His machine, called a differential analyzer, was completed in 1930.

Who is the "Father of the Computer"?

Charles Babbage, a 19th-century British mathematician who designed a mathematical machine capable of processing information, is considered to be the "Father of the Computer."

Is a computer intelligent?

Because computers are capable of calculating at great speeds with perfect accuracy, they are often thought to be intelligent. However, computers are only able to process information given to them by people, who are intelligent beings. Computers never have ideas of their own and so cannot be considered intelligent.

How do computers make pictures?

A computer picture is called a graphic. Artists, architects, engineers, and video game players all use computer graphics. A computer is programmed to change information into graphics when its operator draws, types, or presses buttons or other hand controls. Tiny dots called pixels light up, forming a picture on the screen.

How do computers make music?

Music is an organized collection of sound frequencies a computer can be programmed to reproduce. To reproduce frequencies, the computer sends out electrical signals that represent notes, pitch, timbre, rhythm, and other physical qualities of music. Music made by computer is called electronic music.

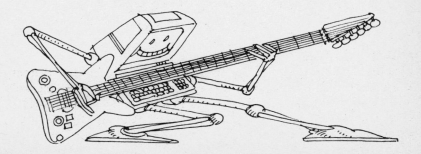

How long will a computer last?

Different parts of the computer have different life spans. The electronic parts, like the microchips, don't wear out. The mechanical parts, like the keyboard, tend to break down first, but can be replaced or fixed. A computer can last a long time, if it is cared for properly.

Can a computer make a mistake?

Computer errors result from feeding wrong information into the machine or from an electrical malfunction of the machine. These errors are called "bugs." The process by which errors are corrected is called "debugging."

How is computer speed measured?

Computers process information so quickly that the speed is not measured in seconds. It is measured in billionths of a second, or nanoseconds.

What language do computers understand?

Computers only understand binary numbers 0 and 1. The programmer uses a special "language" by which the computer translates instructions into the binary system. More than a thousand computer languages based on this binary system are in use today. The most common language used is called BASIC.

How do people communicate with computers?

Most people communicate with a computer by typing information on a keyboard. Some special computers listen to people talk and respond by typing out messages; others respond to the touch of a finger on the screen. There is even a computer which is operated by the user's looking at it. This computer records eye movements and prints the letters at which the person is looking.

FAMOUS COMPUTERS

MARK I This computer was built at Harvard University in 1943. It was over 50 feet long, 10 feet tall, and it weighed five tons. Parts of calculators and accounting machines, along with 500 miles of wire, were used to build this giant. The Mark I was able to multiply a 25-digit number in a matter of seconds.

ENIAC Three times as large as the Mark I, ENIAC (Electronic Numerical Integration and Computer) was about the size of a gym and weighed 30 tons. It was the first electronic computer and had 18,000 electron tubes, 70,000 transistors, and 6,000 switches. The U.S. Army used ENIAC to determine the path of bullets and bombs. ENIAC was built at the University of Pennsylvania in 1946.

EDVAC This was the first computer to use binary arithmetic, store programs, and it was the first to be programmed like today's computers. It was built in 1950 at the University of Pennsylvania.

UNIVAC I Made in the U.S. in 1951, this computer was the first to process letters as well as numbers. It was programmed to calculate the U.S. census. It was also the first computer to be mass produced.

8080 In 1974, the Intel Corporation of California developed this, the first personal size computer, an 8-bit computer on a chip, the first of its kind.

CRAY I The first commercial "supercomputer," Cray I was developed in 1976. It is one of the most powerful computers in the world today, capable of making 200 million calculations in a second. The Cray I makes top secret weapons research calculations for the U.S. government as well as weather forecasts for the U.S. National Weather Bureau.

COMPUTER ACRONYMS AND ABBREVIATIONS

BASIC is an acronym for Beginners All-purpose Symbolic Instruction Code. This computer language is used with many home computers.

Bit is short for binary digit. It's the smallest piece of information a computer can use. Binary means two. A bit is either of the two digits a computer uses, 0 or 1.

CPU stands for Central Processing Unit. The CPU is a chip that is the control center of the computer. It controls all the other chips in the computer.

CRT stands for a Cathode Ray Tube. The CRT is the screen or picture tube in a TV set or computer monitor.

GIGO is an acronym for Garbage In Garbage Out. This is a way of saying that if wrong information is put into a computer, wrong information will come out.

I/O means Input/Output, a basic data processing function that requires the reading of data and producing some output from the data read.

K is the abbreviation for kilobyte or about one thousand bytes of memory. (A byte is an 8-bit sequence of binary digit.) For example, a 64K computer has sixty-four thousand bytes of information.

P.C. is the abbreviation for personal computer, a microcomputer used in the office or home.

RAM is an acronym for Random Access Memory, the memory on a chip where information is stored temporarily.

ROM is an acronym for Read Only Memory, a memory chip which contains instructions for the computer. The information stored in ROM cannot be erased and remains even when the computer is turned off.

Robots

FIVE FACTS ABOUT ROBOTS

1. A robot can be defined as a machine with a computer brain and feedback systems that can be programmed for different kinds of work. Some, but not all, robots are mobile.
2. Robotics is the science and technology of designing, constructing, and maintaining robots.
3. The term *robot* was first used by Karel Capek, a Czechoslovakian playwright, in his play *R.U.R.* In Czech, the word *robota* means worker.
4. Japan is known as the "Island of Robots" because more robots are used in that country than anywhere else in the world.
5. Robots are now built that are the size and shape of large buildings. For example, in Tokyo, Japan, there is a factory-size robot. Inside it, smaller robots work to manufacture other robots. About one hundred humans are on hand to oversee the robot workers.

TYPES OF ROBOTS

Automaton—A machine, like a robot, that works automatically. An automaton doesn't need to be plugged into an electrical outlet, like an appliance, or constantly programmed, like a computer.

Android—A robot built to look and act like a human.

Cyborg—Part human, part robot. TV's "The Six Million Dollar Man" is an example of a Cyborg.

Droid—Robots, that are completely devoted to their human masters. For example, R2D2 and C-3PO from the *Star Wars* movies.

Drone—A worker robot.

Probot—A personal robot for home use. For example, Robby the Robot in the movie, *Forbidden Planet.*

Robotrix—A female robot.

Showbot—An entertainer robot.

A WHO'S WHO OF ROBOTS

Movie Star Robots

GORT
In the 1952 movie, *The Day the Earth Stood Still*, Gort and his master arrive on earth in a spaceship from another planet. They have come to warn humans to stop making atom bombs.

HUEY AND DEWEY
These robots provide the comic relief in the 1972 movie, *Silent Running*.

THE FALSE MARIA
In the 1926 film, *Metropolis*, the False Maria is a robotrix created to look like the human Maria. The False Maria is sent to kill workers and their children, but the real Maria saves them. The False Maria is then burned at the stake and shown to be a robot.

NUMBER FIVE
This soldier robot, created for the army, is hit by lightning and comes alive in *Short Circuit*, a 1986 movie. Number Five develops a mind of its own and decides not to return to the weapons company where it was created.

R2D2 AND C-3PO
These robot stars are featured in the *Star Wars* movies. R2D2 is not humanoid in form. He is four feet tall, glides on the ground, speaks in beeps, toots, and whistles. C-3PO, with its shiny golden skin, is over six feet tall. He is an android who walks, talks (1,000 galactic languages), thinks, and has feelings like a human being.

ROBBY
Robby the Robot plays a central role in *Forbidden Planet* (1956) and *The Invisible Boy* (1957). Robby is now on exhibit at the Planes and Cars Section of the Stars Museum in Buena Vista, California.

ROMAN
This evil, gorilla-like robot starred in the 1953 movie, *Robot Monster*. He played the role of a robot sent to locate and destroy human beings.

SPARKS

This robot was featured in *The Shape of Things to Come*, a 1979 movie about survivors of the destruction of earth. Sparks and the group of survivors manage to reach the moon, but live there in constant danger.

Working Robots

Atom is a robot waiter. He works in a pub on Long Island, New York, where he serves drinks.

Butle is a large truck-like robot who works in a building where nuclear-powered rockets are made. He does jobs which are considered too dangerous for humans.

Blinky delivers mail in the large offices of the U.S. Department of the Interior. He is one of more than 200 robot mail carriers in the U.S.

Herman works for the U.S. Department of Energy. He goes into areas of high radioactivity where humans cannot go. He can lift 160 pounds and drag 500 pounds. His hands can turn valves off and on.

Imp is a professional housecleaner. He vacuums and washes windows. He follows spoken orders indicating where in the house he should clean.

Sico is a robot that works for a robotics company. He promotes the company by attracting attention wherever he goes. He is programmed to move through public places, buy airline tickets with his credit card, and fly first class around the world promoting the company.

Sim One works as an imitation patient at the University of Southern California. There, doctors treat this robot, who is programmed to suffer various heart diseases. He is one of many robots working as patients in the medical world.

Snoopy is a police robot. He shoots tear gas, defuses bombs, and helps police in other dangerous situations. Snoopy works in Oakland, California.

Waldo works for NASA. He is a 50-foot giant robot arm that moves large objects on board the space shuttle.

Dress and Fashion

Kids are fashion trendsetters as well as fashion followers. Here's your chance to learn more about the clothes you wear, what they are made of, and how they were named. Find out some of the superstitions that started certain fashions. And have fun with the names and descriptions of more than twenty different hair styles.

Fashion Around the World

Caftan—Ankle-length garment with long sleeves, usually made of cotton or silk. The style originated in Persia, Turkey, and Russia.

Cowboy hat—A wide-brimmed hat with a large crown worn in the American west.

Djellaba—A long garment with loose sleeves and a hood. Turkish in origin.

Fez—A cone-shaped hat with a flat top and a tassel. Worn in eastern Mediterranean countries.

Kilt—A knee-length pleated skirt worn by Scottish men. The skirt is traditionally of a tartan (plaid) design.

Kimono—A long robe with wide sleeves worn with a wide sash (called an obi). Worn by the Japanese.

Muumuu—A brightly-colored Hawaiian gown that hangs loosely from the shoulders.

Pajamas—Loose, lightweight trousers worn in the Near East.

Parka—A hooded jacket worn by Eskimos.

Sari—A long, wide piece of cloth draped around the head and shoulders and wrapped as a skirt. Worn by women in India.

The Story Behind the Clothes

BIKINI
A two-piece swimsuit named for the shock it caused when it was introduced. Bikini is the name of an island in the Pacific Ocean where the hydrogen bomb was first tested.

CARDIGAN SWEATER
A front-opening sweater, the cardigan was named after James Brudenell, the 7th Earl of Cardigan. A British officer, Brudenell popularized this kind of sweater when he wore one while serving in the Crimean War.

COWBOY BOOTS
These boots were named after the American cowpunchers who began wearing them around 1850. The boots were designed with higher-than-average heels so that they would not slip through the stirrups of a saddle. The stitching on the sides of the boots kept the leather from wrinkling at the ankle.

FISHERMAN'S SWEATER
The fishermen of the Aran Islands, off the coast of Ireland, first wore these cream-colored woolen sweaters. The knitted patterns of the sweaters differed from family to family so that when a drowned sailor washed ashore he could be identified.

JEANS

The first people to wear jeans were the men who prospected for gold in California in the 1850s. One of the prospectors, Levi Strauss, saw the need for sturdy pants for the prospectors. He created the first jeans out of a sturdy cotton. The pockets were secured with metal rivets so that they would not tear. Jean is the name of a strong, twilled cotton fabric.

JAMS

A brand name for brightly-decorated, knee-length surfer trunks. The name was inspired by a cut-off pair of pajamas.

JELLIES

These clear plastic shoes were named because, when worn in the water, they look like jellyfish.

MACKINTOSH

This raincoat, commonly called a "mack," was named after Scots-man Charles Mackintosh, who invented a heavy rubber-coated fabric in 1823.

SNEAKERS

Soft rubber-soled shoes were called sneakers because the person who wore them could sneak around without being heard.

TOPSIDERS

These leather moccasins have a special sole that clings to wet and slick surfaces. Topsiders were first worn on the deck or topside of sailboats and yachts.

TRENCHCOAT

These military-looking coats were designed for officers of the British army who fought in the trenches in World war I.

UNION SUIT

The Union soldiers who fought the U.S. Civil War were the first to wear this one-piece, button-flapped underwear.

Fasteners for Clothing

SNAPS

Snap fasteners were originally created for gloves. Today, snaps can be found on shirts, jeans, and jackets. A Frenchman, Paul-Albert Regnault, invented snaps in 1885.

VELCRO

The inspiration for the velcro fastener was the burrs (sticky, sharp parts) of a woodland plant. In 1948, Swiss engineer George de Mestral returned from a hunting trip to find his clothes covered with burrs. He examined them closely and began the eight-year process of inventing velcro. Velcro fastens in the same way that burrs stick to clothes.

ZIPPERS
Before zippers, people used buttons, laces, and hooks to fasten clothing and footwear. In 1893, a Chicago inventor, Whitcomb Judson, patented the first zipper. He called it a "clasping lock." They were not widely used, because his zippers would often come undone; however, in 1913, Gideon Sundback of Sweden patented an improved zipper like those in use today. These fasteners were named zippers by the B.F. Goodrich Company, who used them in their boots.

Five Fashion Facts and Superstitions

1. The fashion of wearing eye shadow began in ancient times. The Egyptians painted their eyelids to shield their eyes from the sun.

2. Coloring lips with lipstick resulted from the superstitious belief that a red circle painted around the mouth kept the soul inside the body and the devil outside.

3. Hundreds of years ago, sailors pierced their ears and wore earrings because they believed the earrings would keep them from drowning.

4. It is a tradition to wear a wedding band on the fourth finger. This tradition is rooted in the ancient belief that the fourth finger has a nerve that is linked directly to the heart.

5. Umbrellas were first used by royalty in Africa to shade them from the sun. Because umbrellas were associated with the sun god, it was a sacrilege to open them in the shade. This may be the reason why people today consider it unlucky to open an umbrella indoors.

Fiber Guide

WHAT'S IN WHAT WE WEAR

The following guide will help to take the mystery out of clothing labels:

Fiber Name	Fiber Source
Acetate	The wood pulp of trees.
Acrylic	A synthetic made of air, coal, limestone, petroleum, and water.
Angora	Wool made from the hair of angora rabbits and angora goats.
Camel's hair	Wool made from the hair of camels.
Cashmere	Wool made from the hair of Kasmir goats.
Cotton	The pod or boll of the cotton plant.
Linen	The inner stalk of the flax plant.
Nylon	A synthetic made of air, natural gas, petroleum, and water.
Polyester	A synthetic made of air, natural gas, petroleum and water.
Ramie	The inner bark of the boehmeria tree.
Rayon	The wood pulp from pine, hemlock, or spruce trees.
Silk	The cocoon of the silkworm.
Vicuna	Wool made from the hair of llamas.
Wool	The hair of sheep.

Hair

SIX HAIRY TALES

• The ancient Egyptians thought hair was ugly. Both women and men shaved their scalps and wore elaborate wigs. The wigs were worn as a body decoration, not as a substitute for hair.

• Legend has it that the royal tradition of wearing crowns arose because of one ruler's desire to hide his baldness. Ancient Roman Emperor Julius Caesar won his senate's approval to wear a laurel wreath at all times, because he had a balding head and wanted to hide it. Thereafter, kings wore crowns of laurel, jewels, and other prized materials.

• In the 19th century, the United States imported two hundred thousand pounds of human hair, worth about a million dollars, to make hairpieces. At that time, hairpieces were a popular woman's fashion. The hair used to make the hairpieces came mainly from German and French women and girls.

• U.S. Army General George Custer was known for his long blond hair. Shortly before he led his army into battle against the Sioux Indians, he had his hair cut. The Indians, who heard of his haircut, predicted that itmarked the general as a man who would die. At the battle of Little Bighorn (1876), Custer and all his men were killed by the Sioux.

• In the early 1900s, many people in the U.S. treasured locks of hair from loved ones. It was saved and kept in lockets, hair wreaths, watch fobs, and other mementos.

• Among some tribes in Africa, the hairstyle a woman wears is a symbol of her status. Different styles denote whether a woman is married, unmarried, a mother, a mother of twins, or a widow.

WHAT'S YOUR STYLE?

Afro—Closely curled hair worn in round, bushy fullness around the head.

Beehive—Hair pulled to the top of the head in a conical shape with a hole in the center.

Bob—A short, "bowl-on-the-head" cut.

Bouffant—Hair puffed out and kept in place with hair spray.

Braids—Strands of hair braided together and fastened at the ends with rubber bands or barrettes.

Bun—A knot of hair shaped like a bun.

Butch—Bristly short hair often stiffened with wax.

Buzz—Hair cut short with an electric razor so that the scalp shows through.

Chignon—A knot or roll worn at the back of the head or the nape of the neck.

Cornrows—Many rows of tightly braided hair.

Crew cut—A very short haircut, slightly shorter than a *butch*.

Dreadlocks—Long braids of hair first worn by Rastafarians, a religious group of Black Jamaicans.

Ducktail—Hair slicked back on each side to meet in a short "tail" at the back of the head.

Flattop—A *crewcut* with the top flattened out.

French twist—Hair pulled to the back of the head, twisted, and secured with hairpins.

Mohawk—A strip of short hair that runs from the forehead to the nape of the neck. The rest of the head is shaved. A style worn by American Indian tribes of the Northeast.

Pageboy—Shoulder-length hair curled under at the ends.

Pompadour—Hair combed into a high mound above the forehead or in a loose, full roll around the face.

Poodle cut—Short, curly hair that resembles the coat of a poodle.

Queue—A long braid of hair worn hanging at the back of the head.

Shag—A layered haircut, short on top and long on the bottom.

Spikes—Short hair stiffened with hair gel and made to stand up like little spikes.

Spit curl—A spiral curl plastered to the forehead, temple, or cheek. Probably named because it is sometimes stuck down with saliva.

Shingle—Hair trimmed short in layers from the back of the head to the nape of the neck.

Tonsure—Hair shaved at the crown of the head. A style worn by monks in the Roman Catholic church.

Food

Suppose you want to know what kids around the world eat for breakfast. Or, you want to know where it's not unusual for people to eat "thousand year old eggs." You can find this information and other fanciful facts about food in this chapter.

Fun Facts About Food

Facts About Food Consumption in the U.S.

1. The average American who lives to the age of 72 eats 72,135 meals or 35½ tons of food in a lifetime.
2. The average U.S. teenager eats 1,817 pounds of food in a year.
3. In 1986, Americans ate 2.4 billion pounds of chocolate, an average of 8.6 pounds per person.

4. Americans eat more popcorn than any other people in the world. They eat an average of 42 quarts a year. That totals 1.98 billion jumbo containers.

5. According to the U.S. Ice Cream Vendors Association, Americans bought almost five million ice cream bars from ice cream carts and trucks in 1986.

Popcorn: Why It Pops And Other Facts

• Popcorn is a type of corn. It is different from other corn in that its kernels have a tough, waterproof shell which keeps moisture from escaping. When heated, steam builds up inside the kernels until they finally explode. That is how popcorn pops.

• Popcorn is estimated to be 5,600 years old. Its age was determined by archeologists who found traces of popcorn in a cave in New Mexico.

• The Pilgrims tried popcorn at the first Thanksgiving meal. Quadequina, an Indian, brought it as a gift.

• Popcorn was the first "puffed" breakfast cereal. Colonial housewives served popcorn with sugar and cream for breakfast.

• Almost all the popcorn in the world is grown in the U.S. The major popcorn-producing states are Illinois, Iowa, Kansas, Kentucky, Michigan, Missouri, Nebraska, and Ohio.

Five Facts About Ice Cream

1. The ancient Chinese were the first people to add flavoring to snow and eat this icy concoction.

2. Marco Polo returned to Europe from China in the 13th century with a recipe for ice milk.

3. Thomas Jefferson popularized ice cream, his favorite dessert, in the United States during his presidency (1801-1809).

4. Ice cream cones were invented at the St. Louis World's Fair in 1904. A vendor selling ice cream ran out of dishes. A pastry-seller rolled up one of his wafers and asked the vendor to put ice cream in it. Together, they sold the first ice cream cones.

5. The immigrants who arrived on Ellis Island, New York, in the early 20th century were served ice cream at their first American meal. Some of them were confused by the new food and spread it on their bread.

Six Facts About Pizza

1. Pizza means "pie" in Italian. It is a yeast dough covered with tomato sauce and topped with cheese and meat or vegetables, and then baked. Without the toppings to weigh it down, the bread would puff up when it is baked.

2. Pizza was created over 500 years ago by the women of Naples, Italy. The Duke of Naples, who lived in the 1400s, is credited with popularizing pizza and its many varied toppings.

3. The first pizza made with tomatoes and cheese was created for Queen Margherita of Italy in 1889. The pizzamaker, Raffaele Esposito, used ingredients that matched colors of the Italian flag: tomatoes (red), mozzarella cheese (white), and basil leaves (green).

4. The first pizza parlor in America was opened in New York City in 1905 by Gennaro Lombardi. Pizza was originally considered to be a foreign food and was found only in Italian neighborhoods.

5. American soldiers popularized pizza in America. After World War II, the soldiers who served in Italy brought their taste for pizza back to the U.S.

6. Pizzamakers started to spin the dough in the air during the 1930s. The gesture of spinning pizza dough is for show only; it is not a function of pizzamaking.

Favorite Foods of Storybook Characters

1. Alice in Wonderland liked strawberry tarts.
2. Dorothy of *The Wizard of Oz* liked porridge and scrambled eggs.
3. Heidi liked toasted cheese sandwiches.
4. Homer Price liked doughnuts.
5. Tom Sawyer liked fried fish.

Eight Nicknames For Doughnuts

bellysinkers	burl cakes
doorknobs	cymballs
dunkers	fried cakes
flatcakes	sinkers

Six Vegetables That Are Really Fruits

1. Eggplant
2. Tomatoes
3. Squash
4. Okra
5. Cucumbers
6. Pumpkins

Five Bread Facts

1. The first bread was made in China.
2. The Egyptians were the first to make sourdough bread. They discovered that if they let the dough ferment before baking it, the result was raised bread.
3. The first public bakeries were in Greece.
4. Columbus brought sourdough bread with him when he sailed to the New World.
5. The French Revolution was sparked by a bread riot.

Five Myths About Food

1. An apple a day keeps the doctor away.
2. Honey is less fattening than sugar.
3. Toasted bread is lower in calories than untoasted bread.
4. Fish is a brain food.
5. Lemons make the blood thin.

Five Kinds of Sandwiches

1. **Club sandwich.** This kind of sandwich consists of three pieces of toast and two layers of filling. Usually, one layer of filling is lettuce and turkey; the second layer is bacon and tomato. Also known as a triple decker.

2. **Hero.** So-named because of the "hero-sized" appetite needed to consume this large sandwich. The ingredients include cold cuts, cheese, onion, lettuce, and tomato on a long thin loaf of bread. The hero is also known as a hoagie, sub, poor boy, torpedo, or wedge.

3. **Open-faced sandwich.** This sandwich is made with one slice of bread or toast, which serves as a base for slices of meat, chicken, or turkey covered with gravy. Also called hot sandwiches.

4. **Tea sandwich.** This is a regular sandwich, but the crusts have been removed and the sandwich sliced in four quarters. Tea Sandwiches are usually served at afternoon teas.

5. **Zoo sandwich.** Most often served at children's parties, these sandwiches are made of bread and a favorite filling. Cookie cutters are used to cut the sandwiches into the shapes of animals.

Fifteen Ways to Prepare Eggs

1. **Baked**—Eggs are taken out of the shell, put on toast, and cooked in the oven.

2. **Coddled**—Eggs in their shells are put in boiling water, covered, and removed from heat. They steep in the hot water for six to eight minutes.

3. **Deviled**—Hard-boiled eggs have the shells removed and are cut in half. The yolks are removed and mixed with mayonnaise and other seasonings. The yolk mixture is spread on the egg white halves.

4. **Eggs Benedict**—A poached egg served on a toasted English muffin with a slice of ham and a creamy sauce, called Hollandaise.

5. **Egg in a Bag**—An egg is broken into a paper bag. The bag is held by a stick over the coals of a campfire.

6. **Hard-boiled**—Eggs in their shells are placed in a pot of cold water. The water is brought to a boil and the eggs are cooked for 10 minutes.

7. **Hole in the Bread**—The center is removed from a slice of bread. An egg is cracked over the bread so that the yolk falls into the bread hole. The bread and egg are fried.

8. **Omelette**—A scrambled egg mixture that is sauteed in butter. The omelette is often filled with cheese, vegetables, or meat as it is cooking.

9. **Over easy**—An egg cracked into a pan and fried lightly on both sides.

10. **Pickled**—Hard-boiled eggs are taken out their shells, put in a seasoned vinegar brine, and refrigerated. They are eaten cold.

11. **Poached**—Eggs are removed from their shells and cooked gently in boiling water.

12. **Scrambled**—Eggs are beaten with milk and stirred while frying in butter.

13. **Shirred**—Eggs in their shells are placed in a pan of water and baked in the oven.

14. **Soft-boiled**—Eggs in their shells are placed in a pot of cold water. The water is brought to a boil and the eggs are cooked for two to three minutes.

15. **Sunnyside up**—Eggs are cracked open into a pan and fried with the yolk facing up.

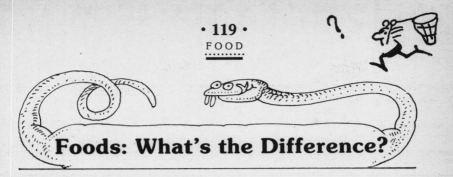

Foods: What's the Difference?

APPLE CIDER AND APPLE JUICE

Apples are ground up and pressed to extract juice. Before it ferments, apple juice is known as sweet cider. Once it ages and ferments, it is known as hard cider.

BAGELS AND BIALYS

A bagel is a doughnut-shaped roll which is boiled in water and then baked. A bialy is a baked roll with a depression in its center. bialys are often onion flavored. Bagels are made in a variety of flavors, including raisin, pumpernickel, onion, poppy seed, and sesame seed.

BUTTER AND MARGARINE

Butter is made by churning milk, cream, or a combination of both until a solid product results. Margarine is a butter substitute made from vegetable, corn, or other oils, mixed with milk and salt. It was created in 1869 by a chemist, Hippolyte Mège-Mouries, for the French government which wanted a cheap butter substitute for its armed forces. Originally, margarine consisted of processed animal fat, called tallow.

CHOCOLATE, COCOA, CAROB

Chocolate and cocoa are both made from the cocoa beans of the cocoa tree. When the beans are melted, they form an oily liquid called chocolate liquor. Cocoa, a powder, is made by removing some of the oil or cocoa butter. Chocolate is the pure form of cocoa liquor. Both chocolate and cocoa are naturally bitter and are sweetened with sugar.

Carob is made from the pods of the carob tree; it is often used as a chocolate substitute. Unlike cocoa beans, which are bitter, carob pods are naturally sweet.

HOMINY AND GRITS

Hominy is made from hulled, degermed corn. The finest-ground hominy is called grits. It is eaten as a breakfast cereal or as a side dish with other meals. Whole kerneled hominy is called pearl hominy. It is eaten with dinner as a rice or potato substitute.

ICE CREAM AND SHERBET

Ice cream is made from fresh, condensed or dried milk products blended with gelatin, sweeteners, and a multitude of flavorings. Ice cream contains from 10 percent to 20 percent butterfat.

Sherbet is made from water, sweeteners, flavorings, and other ingredients, such as egg whites, milk, and gelatin. It is almost fat free, but is higher in sugar content than ice cream.

JAM AND JELLY

Both spreads are made from fruit and sugar. Jelly is made from the juice of fruit. Jam is made from the pulp of fruit.

SELTZER AND CLUB SODA

Both seltzer and club soda are made from filtered and carbonated tap water. Minerals, including salt, are added to club soda but not to seltzer.

The Inside Story on Foods

FIVE FOOD ADDITIVES

Any chemicals added to foods to preserve, enrich, or improve them are additives. Food manufacturers use more than 3,000 kinds of additives. To find out what kinds of additives are in the foods you eat, read the list of ingredients on the food packages in your home or at the grocery store. Five additives, with reasons why they are used, are listed below.

1. **Preservatives**, such as salt, prevent the growth of bacteria that cause foods to spoil.
2. **Nutritional supplements,** such as minerals and vitamins, are added to make food more nourishing.
3. **Flavoring agents** include sugar, spices, and fruit flavors, as well as synthetic flavors. These are added to make food taste better.
4. **Coloring agents** make foods look more appetizing. For example, yellow coloring is added to margarine to make it look like butter.
5. **Emulsifiers** keep the ingredients in foods mixed and held together. For example, they give ice cream its creamy texture.

FOODS AND FLAVORINGS

Bologna   A sausage made from ground pork, beef, and milk seasonings.

Caviar   The eggs of the female sturgeon fish.

Chili Powder   A blend of spices that includes hot chili peppers, garlic, oregano, cloves and cumin.

Chives   The long thin leaves of this plant in the onion family.

Cinnamon   The dried inner bark of the cinnamon tree. It is usually ground into powder but is also available in sticks.

Horseradish   The root of the horseradish plant, which is grated.

Marshmallow   A spongy white candy made of sugar, gelatin, corn syrup, and beaten egg whites. It is named after an edible plant called marshmallow.

Mustard   Prepared mustard spread, made by grinding mustard seed, a spice, and blending it with vinegar and other seasonings. Mustard seed may be yellow, brown, or black, depending on the type.

Olives   Olives are the fruits of the olive tree. They must be cured in brine to be eaten.

Paprika   Ground red chili peppers which range in taste from mild to pungent.

Pickles   Cucumbers that have been preserved in vinegar and spices.

Prunes   Plums which have been dehydrated.

Raisins   Grapes which have been dried by the sun or by artificial heat.

Sour Cream   Not spoiled cream, but cream to which harmless bacteria have been added.

Soy sauce   A blend of fermented soybeans, wheat, yeast, salt, and sugar.

Tofu   White soybeans which have been cooked, mashed, and pressed into cakes. Also called bean curd.

Vanilla   A flavoring made from the beans of the vanilla plant. Vanilla extract used in cooking contains vanilla, alcohol, and water.

Yogurt   Semisolid milk which is made more acidic by adding harmless bacteria.

Sugar By Any Other Name Is Still Sugar

Sugar is a sweet-tasting carbohydrate that is extracted from the juices of certain plants. The most common form of sugar is derived from sugar cane and sugar beets. Sugar may appear in your food under a different name. Below are some of the other names for sugar.

Barley malt syrup	Maltose
Brown sugar	Maple syrup
Corn syrup	Molasses
Dextrose	Raisin syrup
Fructose	Raw sugar
Honey	Sorghum
Lactose	Turbinado sugar

Sugar In Your Food

A sampling of foods and their sugar content is listed below.

Food	Teaspoons of Sugar	Food	Teaspoons of Sugar
Brownie (2-inch square)	3	Plain granola bar	2
Chocolate bar (2 oz.)	7	Raisins (¼ cup)	4
Chocolate milk (8 oz.)	6	Sherbet (½ cup)	7
Doughnut	4	Soft drink (12 oz.)	9
Ice cream (½ cup)	5½	Sugared cereal (1 cup)	4
Orange juice (4 oz., frozen)	2½	Yogurt, fruit-flavored (8 oz.)	6

NUTRITION IN KIDS' FAVORITE FOODS

Food	Calories	Cholesterol*	Protein*	Fat*
Vanilla Ice Cream (1 cup)	290	30.2	5.7	16.2
Hamburger	252	29.0	14.0	9.0
Hot dog	273	23.0	11.0	15.0
Pizza (1 slice, cheese)	718	97.8	37.6	19.6
Macaroni & Cheese (homemade, 1 cup)	430	40.2	16.8	22.2
Apple (small)	58	14.5	--	--
Tuna fish sandwich (on white bread)	278	25.8	11.0	14.2
Chicken noodle soup (bowl of canned)	152	20.6	8.6	3.9
Grilled cheese sandwich	338	38.2	17.0	18.5
Peanut butter & jelly sandwich	374	50.0	12.3	15.1
Bacon (4 pieces)	692	--	8.7	72.4
Watermelon (1 slice)	156	38.4	--	--
Jello (½ cup)	97	23.5	1.7	--
Carrots (small, 2 raw)	42	9.7	1.1	--
Chocolate bar (Hershey's)	706	84.0	5.8	44.2
Doughnut	111	12.2	1.1	6.8

*Measured in grams.

Typical Menu For
U.S. Space Shuttle Flights*

Day 1

Peaches (T)
Beef patty (R)
Scrambled eggs (R)
Bran flakes (R)
Cocoa (B)
Orange drink (B)

Frankfurters (T)
Turkey tetrazzini (R)
Bread (I) (NF)
Bananas (FD)
Almond crunch bar (NF)
Apple drink (B)

Shrimp cocktail (R)
Beef steak (T) (I)
Rice pilaf (R)
Broccoli au gratin (R)
Fruit cocktail (T)
Butterscotch pudding (T)
Grape drink (B)

Day 2

Applesauce (T)
Beef jerky (NF)
Granola (R)
Breakfast roll (I) (NF)
Chocolate, instant breakfast (B)
Orange-grapefruit drink (B)

Corned beef (T) (I)
Asparagus (R)
Bread (I) (NF)
Pears (T)
Peanuts (NF)
Lemonade (B)

Beef w/barbeque sauce (T)
Cauliflower w/cheese (R)
Green beans w/mushrooms (R)
Lemon cookies (NF)
Pecan cookies (NF)
Cocoa (B)

The abbreviations in parentheses indicate the type of food.

(T) Thermostabilized—Heat processed "off the shelf" foods in tins or pouches.

(I) Irradiated—Foods preserved by exposing to ionizing radiation and packed in foil laminated pouches.

(IM) Intermediate Moisture—Dried foods such as dried apricots packed in plastic pouches.

(FD) Freeze Dried—Foods prepared to eat, then frozen and then dried. Freeze-dried fruits can be eaten as is; others require water.

Day 3

Dried peaches (M)
Sausage (R)
Scrambled eggs (R)
Cornflakes (R)
Cocoa (B)
Orange-pineapple drink (B)

Ham (T) (I)
Cheese spread (T)
Bread (I) (NF)
Green beans and broccoli (R)
Crushed pineapple (T)
Shortbread cookies (NF)
Cashews (NF)
Tea w/lemon and sugar (B)

Cream of mushroom soup (R)
Smoked turkey (T) (I)
Mixed Italian vegetables (R)
Vanilla pudding (T) (R)
Strawberries (R)
Tropical punch (B)

Day 4

Dried apricots (M)
Breakfast roll (I) (NF)
Granola w/blueberries (R)
Vanilla instant breakfast (B)
Grapefruit drink (B)

Ground beef w/pickle sauce (T)
Noodles and chicken (R)
Stewed tomatoes (T)
Pears (FD)
Almonds (NF)
Strawberry drink (B)

Tuna (T)
Macaroni and cheese (R)
Peas w/butter sauce (R)
Peach ambrosia (R)
Chocolate pudding (T) (R)
Lemonade (B)

(R) Rehydratable—Dried foods and cereals that are rehydrated with water produced by the Shuttle Orbiter's Fuel Cell System. Packed in plastic containers with a system for water injection.

(NF) Natural Form—Foods such as nuts and cookies packed in plastic pouches.

(B) Beverages—Dry powder mixes packed in rehydratable containers.

Foods From Around The World

UNUSUAL FOODS

BIRD'S NEST SOUP
This gourmet Chinese food is made from the nest of a bird called the Asian swift. The bird uses its saliva to glue together twigs for its nest. This hardened saliva, which is rich in protein, is removed from the nest to make the soup.

DIRT
Dirt-eating is common among some tribes of Nigeria. It is also eaten by some rural people in Mississippi and other southern states. The dirt is dug from a clay bank; then it is baked and seasoned with vinegar and salt before eating.

GRASSHOPPERS
Grasshoppers are prepared by removing the arms and legs and frying the bodies. Richer in protein than beef, grasshoppers were once eaten by the North American Indians of the Rocky Mountains. Today, grasshoppers are eaten in Africa, Australia, Japan, New Guinea, and South America.

KANGAROO
The aborigines of Australia prize kangaroo meat. When a kangaroo is caught, it is roasted whole over an open pit.

SEAWEED
Seaweed is the wild plant that grows in the underwater fields of the ocean. It is a popular food in Japan where a variety of seaweeds are used in soups and salads, wrapped around rice, or simply toasted. Seaweed contains valuable vitamins and minerals.

THOUSAND YEAR OLD EGGS
A before-meal treat in China, thousand year old eggs are not ancient eggs. They are usually duck's eggs, which are buried for about eight weeks in a special kind of clay. After they are dug up, the outsides are black and the insides are bright blue and green. These eggs are eaten raw and have a somewhat fishy taste.

STREET FOOD

In many cities of the world, vendors sell food on the street, and busy people can eat on the run. The following is a list of some of the foods available on the streets of New York City.

Baked potatoes
Frankfurters
Fresh fruit
Ice cream/ices
Hot pretzels
Nuts and dried fruits

Chestnuts
Roasted peanuts
Sausage and pepper sandwiches
Shish kebabs (skewered roast meat)
Sliced barbecued pork
Knishes

AMERICAN FOODS WITH FOREIGN NAMES

Although they sound as if they come from other countries, all of the foods below were created in the United States.

Chili con carne
Chop Suey
Cioppino (fish stew)
English muffins
French fries

Liederkranz cheese
Russian dressing
Swiss steak
Vichyssoise (potato and
    leek soup served cold)

Old World and New World Foods

When Europeans first came to America, they carried seeds, plants, and livestock on their ships. Slaves who were brought to America often carried seed in their pockets. For this reason, the foods that were imported are still being grown in America today. We may think of them as American foods, but they originated in Europe and Africa. Some of the foods brought from the Old World to the New World are listed below.

Apples	Carrots	Lettuce	Pears
Beef (cows)	Cow's Milk	Okra	Rye
Black-eyed peas	Cow's milk cheese	Oranges	Watermelons
Cabbage	Lentils	Peaches	Wheat

Foods eaten in America by the native Indians and early settlers were taken back to Europe where they became popular. Some of the foods brought from the New World back to the Old World are listed below.

Chili peppers   Maple syrup   Squash
Corn   Peanuts   Tomatoes
Dried cod   Potatoes   Turkeys
                    Sweet potatoes

KIDS' BREAKFASTS AROUND THE WORLD

Country	Typical Breakfast
Argentina	Steak, eggs, milk.
Chile	Bread, butter, coffee (most often with sugar and lots of milk).
China	Rice porridge, dried pork, Chinese pickle (cucumber in sugar and salt), soybean juice or milk.
England	Boiled eggs, sausages, toasted bread strips, tea.
France	Bread and butter, hot chocolate.
Israel	Bread with butter and honey, sliced cucumbers, sliced tomatoes, juice.
Italy	Bread with a chocolate butter spread, hot milk with a dash of coffee.
Japan	Toasted seaweed dipped in soy sauce, rice, hot tea.
Philippines	Fried rice and vegetables with coffee poured over it.
Puerto Rico	Cooked cornmeal or oatmeal with hot milk poured over it, coffee.
Spain	Toast, crackers, or biscuits served with milk.
Sudan	A dish of warm fava beans and tomatoes, onions, and goat cheese with a lemon and oil dressing, hot tea with milk.
Switzerland	A hard roll with butter and jam, milk or hot chocolate.
Turkey	Bread with butter and jam, cured olives, goat cheese, hot milk.

U.S.S.R.	Hot oat or wheat cereal, boiled eggs (or bologna sandwiches in place of these first two), hot chocolate or tea with milk.
West Germany	Cold meats, bread, hot tea.

Famous Meals in History

The Last Supper

• The Last Supper was a Passover meal called the seder which commemorates the Israelites' freedom from their enslavement in Egypt.

• The 13 guests included Jesus and his 12 disciples.*

• The supper was prepared by the disciples and eaten in the upstairs room of a friend's house.

• The meal consisted of roast lamb, bitter herbs, charoseth (a pastelike mixture of apples, nuts, cinnamon, and wine), dates, figs, almonds in syrup, matzoh (unleavened bread), and wine. Although often depicted in paintings, oranges were not part of the meal.

The disciples were Peter, James, John, Andrew, Philip, Bartholomew, Matthew, Thomas, James the Lesser, Thaddeus, Simon, and Judas.

The First Thanksgiving

• The Pilgrims entertained 92 Indian guests at the 1621 event.

• The first Thanksgiving meal was a breakfast.

• Boiled eel, lobster, roast pigeon, and stuffed cod were served at the meal.

• The Indians brought turkeys, pumpkins, corn, sweet potatoes, and cranberries to the celebration.

• The Pilgrims had their first taste of popcorn, which was given to them by the Indian brave, Quadequina, brother of Chief Massasoit.

Inventions

Are you a budding inventor or do you know someone who is? In this chapter, you will read about other kids who were inventors, famous inventions that changed the way people live, and unbelievable inventions just for pets.

U.S Patented Inventions

A patent is a type of license which protects a person's invention. Each year, more than 100,000 people believe they have an invention which should be protected by a patent. Anyone may apply for a patent. To obtain a patent, the inventor must submit a model of the invention, a written description, and an application fee. Since 1790, the year the patent law was passed, over four million patents have been granted. A patent gives the inventor "the right to exclude others from making, using, or selling the invention throughout the United States" for 17 years.

Below are some of the most interesting patented inventions and the inventors' names. Inventors who have been named to the National Inventors Hall of Fame are noted by a star.

For more information on patents, write to:

U.S. Patent and Trademark Offices
Washington, D.C. 20231

The National Inventors Hall of Fame
2021 Jefferson Davis Highway
Arlington, VA 22202

INVENTIONS A-Z

Invention	*Inventor*	*Year Issued*
Air conditioner	Willis Carrier*	1911
Airplane with motor	Orville Wright;* Wilbur Wright*	1903
Aluminum manufacture	Charles Hall*	1886
Aspirin	Hermann Dresser	1889
Automobile (gasoline)	Charles Duryea	1892
Ballpoint pen	John J. Loud	1888
Barbed wire	Joseph Glidden	1874
Cash register	James Ritty	1879
Cosmetics (modern)	George Washington Carver	1925
Cotton gin	Eli Whitney*	1794
Diesel engine	Rudolf Diesel*	1895
Elevator (with braking device)	Elisha Otis	1852
Electric razor	Jacob Schick	1928
Frozen foods, packaged	Clarence Birdseye	1930
Icemaking machine	John Gorrie	1851
Ironing board	Sarah Boone	1892

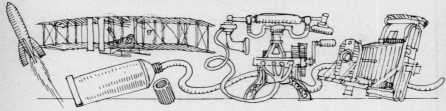

Invention	Inventor	Year Issued
Laser	Arthur Schawlow; Charles H. Townes*	1958
Matches (friction)	John Walker	1827
Microphone	Emile Berliner	1877
Motion picture projector	Thomas A. Edison*	1892
Motor (alternating current)	Nikola Tesla*	1892
Neutronic reactor	Enrico Fermi;* Leo Szilard	1955
Nylon	DuPont Laboratory	1937
Polaroid film	Edwin Land*	1948
Phonograph	Thomas A. Edison*	1877
Photo film (transparent)	George Eastman	1884
Radio amplifier	Lee de Forest*	1906
Radio (FM)	Edwin Armstrong*	1933
Reaper	Cyrus McCormick*	1834
Refrigeration	Jacob Perkins	1834
Revolver	Samuel Colt	1836
Rocket engine	Robert H. Goddard*	1926
Rubber, vulcanized	Charles Goodyear*	1839
Safety pin	Walter Hunt	1849
Sewing machine	Elias Howe	1846
Steamboat	Robert Fulton	1803
Submarine (even keel)	Simon Lake	1894
Suspenders	Samuel Clemens (Mark Twain)	1871
Tape measure	Alvin J. Fellows	1868
Telegraph signs	Samuel F. Morse*	1840

Invention	Inventor	Year Issued
Telegraph, wireless	Guglielmo Marconi	1895
Telephone	Alexander Graham Bell*	1876
Toothpaste tube	John Rand	1841
Television	Philo T. Farnsworth	1930
Transistor	John Burdeen;* William Shockley;* Walter Brattain*	1947
Typewriter	C. Latham Sholes; Carlos Glidden; Samuel W. Soule	1867
Vacuum cleaner	Ives McGaffey	1869
Vaseline	Robert Chesebrough	1872
Videotape recorder	Charles P. Ginsberg; Shelby Anderson, Jr.; Ray Dolby	1960
Washing machine	Chester Stone	1827
Xerography (instant copying)	Chester Carlson*	1938
X-ray tube	William Collidge*	1913

History-Making U.S. Inventors

• **Thomas Edison** has patented the most inventions. Among his 1,093 inventions are the phonograph, the motion-picture projector, and the incandescent electric lamp.

• **Samuel Hopkins** received the first patent issued under the U.S. Patent Bill in 1790. The patent, which was signed by President George Washington, was for the making of potash, a chemical used to make soap.

• **Samuel Briggs, Sr., and Samuel Briggs, Jr.,** were the first father and son to be given a patent for their invention. They invented a nail-making machine in 1791.

• **Mary Kies** was the first woman to patent an invention. In 1809, she patented her "Weaving Straw with Silk or Thread," a device for making fabric.

• **Henry Blair** was the first black patentee. He was issued a patent in 1834 for a "Corn Planter."

• **Abraham Lincoln** was the only president to have patented an invention. In 1849, Lincoln patented a device for buoying ships over shoals.

• **Robert Patch** was the youngest inventor. He was issued a patent for a toy truck in 1962. Robert was five years old.

More Inventions

EIGHT VERY POPULAR INVENTIONS

CHEWING GUM

The use of chewing gum dates back to the ancient Mayan Indians of Central America. The Mayans chewed the chicle, or sap, of the apodilla plant. The American Indians who lived in New England chewed the resin of spruce trees. In 1848, spruce-tree resin was marketed as a chewing gum by an American, J. Curtis. Soon afterward, T. Adams, another American, imported and sold chicle for chewing. Because chicle held the flavors added to it better than resin, it became a more popular chewing gum. In 1869, William F. Semple was granted the first patent for his chicle chewing gum.

DRINKING STRAW

It seems like a simple idea, but it was not until 1888 that anyone thought to patent the invention of the drinking straw. Marvin C. Stone of Washington, D.C., was awarded a patented for hand-rolled straws made of wax-coated paper.

FRISBEE
The first Frisbees were empty pork cans, pounded flat. The students of Yale University first started throwing these empty discs around in 1947. In 1968, American Fred Morrison patented the plastic version of the can known as the Frisbee.

TOILET, FLUSH
The ancient Minoan civilization of Crete used running water to flush waste material circa 2000 B.C.

UMBRELLA
People have used umbrellas for thousands of years as protection from sun as well as rain. In some cultures, umbrellas were also used to signify wealth and rank by their color and style. It is thought that the ancient Chinese were the first to make umbrellas.

YO-YO
The people of the Philippines used the yo-yo thousands of years ago as a deadly weapon for fighting and hunting. In 1929, Donald Duncan watched a Filipino demonstrate tricks with a yo-yo in California. Duncan was inspired to manufacture the yo-yo as a toy.

JIGSAW PUZZLE
The jigsaw puzzle began as a game for teaching geography. In 1760, Englishman John Spilsbury glued a map of England to a piece of wood; he then cut up the map into pieces by boundary lines of countries. He thought children would learn their geography better by playing the game of putting the pieces together again.

SILLY PUTTY
Silly Putty was created by researchers at General Electric to replace rubber. It was not an adequate substitute for rubber, so it was abandoned but not discarded. In 1947, American Peter Hodgson bought $147 worth of the soft, elastic substance from General Electric. He went on to package it, name it Silly Putty, and sell it as a toy.

INVENTIONS BY KIDS

BRAILLE
Fifteen-year-old Louis Braille, a blind boy from France, invented a system of writing which has been used by millions of blind people the world over. While attending a special school for the blind in the 1820s, he developed a system of raised dots that could be felt and thus "read" by blind people. Today, there are Braille wristwatches and Braille musical scores.

MAN-MADE DYE
Eighteen-year-old William Perkin of England invented synthetic (man-made) dyes in 1856. Before Perkin's invention, all clothing was dyed by natural dyes from plants, animals, and earth. The color of Perkins' first chemical dye was mauveine (purple) and was made from coal tar.

EARMUFFS
Fifteen-year-old Chester Greenwood of the United States invented earmuffs in 1873. While ice-skating, his ears became cold and turned blue. He made his "ear protectors" by twisting wire into two hoops and having his grandmother sew cloth into them. In 1877, he patented "Chester's Champion Ear Protectors."

TOY TRUCK
Five-year-old Robert Patch is the youngest known inventor. In 1962, he was issued a U.S. patent for his toy truck which was designed to be taken apart and put back together. Another feature of his truck was that several types of trucks could be made from one truck.

"COOLING FORK"
A fourteen-year-old Belgian boy, Eric Van Paris, invented a "Cooling Fork" in 1982. He wanted to find a way for kids to eat hot food. The device is made from a rubber squeeze bulb connected by a tube to a fork. Air forced through the tube cools the hot food on the fork.

PECULIAR INVENTIONS FOR PETS

BIRD DIAPER
Bertha Dlugi wanted her bird to fly freely around her house without making a mess. In 1956, she patented her invention, a bird diaper.

DOG GLASSES
Denise Lemiere, a French opthamologist, invented glasses to protect dogs' eyes from wind and dust as well as to correct their eyesight. In 1975, Dr. Lemiere patented her invention.

PET CAR SEAT
People can safely transport their pets by car with this invention. Paul Rux was issued a patent for the pet car seat in 1983.

TOOTHBRUSH FOR DOGS
A special toothbrush designed for dogs' teeth and gums was patented by Bird Eyer in 1961. Bird Eyer was a judge for animal shows and he noticed that many dogs did not have clean teeth.

TRAINING PANTS FOR DOGS
These pants were invented to help housebreak dogs. David Hersh was given the patent for these specially-designed training pants in 1965.

Language

Who first said "The moon is made of green cheese?" What do stone skippers call a stone that sinks without skipping? What are pogonophobics afraid of? The answers to these questions, plus lots of other fun and useful facts about language can be found in this chapter. Also featured are anagrams, acronyms, proverbs, measurements, numbers, and CB slang. It won't be a *peck* of trouble and it won't take you a *centillion* years!

The Spoken Word

- About 3,000 different languages are spoken in the world.
- The English language is spoken in more countries of the world than any other language.
- The Chinese language (Mandarin) is spoken by the greatest number of people.
- On the average, a person speaks about 4,000 words a day.

- The longest word in the world is an old Greek word for meat stew. It has 182 letters in it. The English translation is:

  Lopadotemachoselachogaleokranioleipsanodrimhypotrimmatos-
  ilphioparaomelitokatakechymenokichlepikossyphophattoper-
  isteralektryonoptekephalliokigklopeleiolaoiosiraiobaphetragan-
  opterygon.

- The shortest word is *a*.
- One of the most difficult tongue twisters in the English language is "The sixth sick sheik's sixth sheep's sick".
- The English language has more words than any other world language: 490,000 words.
- The word spoken most often is *I*.

Words and Expressions

THE STORY BEHIND FIVE POPULAR EXPRESSIONS

Give someone the cold shoulder. To ignore someone. In medieval days, knights were greeted at the castle with a warm meal. Unwanted visitors were given a cold shoulder of mutton to eat.

Get up on the wrong side of the bed. To wake up grumpy. In ancient Rome, people believed that getting out of bed on the left side was unlucky and would result in an unpleasant day.

Lay an egg. To be a failure. In the early years of baseball, when a zero was shown on the scoreboard, it was referred to as a goose egg.

Putting on the dog. Acting stuck-up. At the turn of the century, Americans who wanted to impress people bought expensive dogs to sit on their laps. This was an imitation of a custom among the high society of England at the time.

Let the cat out of the bag. To reveal a secret unintentionally. Years ago, people sold small pigs in bags at county fairs. Sometimes a dishonest seller would put a cat rather than a pig in the bag. When the bag was opened, the secret was revealed.

PORTMANTEAU WORDS

A portmanteau word is one which has been made up from two words.

Brunch	Breakfast and lunch
Chortle	Chuckle and snort
Mimsy	Miserable and flimsy
Slithy	Slimy and lithe
Squawk	Squeak and squall

STONE-SKIPPING LANGUAGE

Pittipats—The short skips at the end of a run.

Plinks—Long skips.

Plunker—A stone that sinks without skipping.

Skronker—A stone that never lands.

MAGICIANS' LINGO

Below are words used by magicians to distract the audience from the trickery:

Abracadabra!
Alakazam!
Hocus Pocus!
Presto!

EUPHEMISMS

Euphemisms are pleasant-sounding expressions which are substituted for unpleasant words or expressions.

"Birthday suit"	Nude
"Blow your fuse"	To lose your temper
"Have a hollow leg"	To eat excessively
"Lay out in lavender"	Angry desire to knock someone down
"Put on airs"	Act in a superior way

ACRONYMS

An acronym is a word formed by the first letters of a series of words.

Laser—Light amplication by stimulated emission of radiation

Radar—Radar detecting and ranging

Scuba—Self-contained underwater breathing apparatus

Sonar—Sound navigation range

Snafu—Situation normal all fouled up

PROVERBS AND WISE SAYINGS FROM AROUND THE WORLD

African	When elephants battle, it is the grass that suffers.
American	A friend in need is a friend indeed.
British	A fool and his money are soon parted.
Chinese	The ripest fruit will not fall into your mouth.
Czech	A handful of friends is better than a wagon of gold.
French	As you made your bed, so must you lie in it.
German	The tooth often bites the tongue, and yet they stay together.
Norwegian	A lazy man works twice.
Scottish	Live and let live.
Spanish	The closed mouth swallows no flies.

PHOBIAS—THE LANGUAGE OF FEAR

Fear of:

Animals	Zoophobia
Beards	Pogonophobia
Being dirty	Automysophobia
Being stared at	Scopophobia
Crossing a bridge	Gephydrophobia
Dogs	Cynophobia
Everything	Pantophobia
Fire	Pyrophobia
Food	Sitophobia
Ghosts	Phasmophobia
Going to bed	Clinophobia

Fear of:

Heights	Acrophobia
Mice	Musophobia
Mirrors	Eisoptrophobia
Monsters	Teratophobia
Night	Nyctophobia
Punishment	Poinephobia
School	Scholionophobia
Shadows	Sciophobia
Smothering	Pnigerphobia
Strangers	Xenophobia
Thunder	Tonitrophobia
Water	Hydrophobia

ANAGRAMS OF FIRST NAMES

Anagrams are words scrambled to make other words.

Boys		Girls	
Name	**Anagram**	**Name**	**Anagram**
Alfred	flared	Clare	clear
Andrew	wander	Erin	rein
Brian	brain	Glenda	dangle
Daniel	nailed	Kay	yak
Dennis	sinned	Lois	soil
Earl	real	Mary	army
Eric	rice	Melissa	aimless
Gerald	glared	Rose	sore
Leon	lone	Ruth	hurt
Steven	events	Teresa	teaser

THE NAME "JOHN" IN OTHER COUNTRIES

Italy	Giovanni
Germany	Hans
Scotland	Ian
Russia	Ivan
France	Jean
Spain	Juan
Ireland	Sean

TOASTS AROUND THE WORLD

Brazil	Viva
China	Nien nien nue
England	Cheers
France	A votre santé
Germany	Prosit
Hawaii	Okole maluna
India	Jaikind
Italy	Salute
Israel	L'chayim
Japan	Banzai
Poland	Vivat
Scandinavia	Skoal
Spain	Salud

ORIGINS OF FAMOUS PHRASES

Don't Give up the Ship.
This is a paraphrase of the final order given by Captain James Lawrence when his ship the *Chesapeake* was captured by the British in the War of 1812. Before he died of a wound, Captain Lawrence said, "Tell the men to fire faster and not to give up the ship; fight till she sinks."

A horse! a horse! my kingdom for a horse!
William Shakespeare made these words famous in his historical play, *Richard III*. At the end of the play, King Richard III dies in battle at Bosworth Field, England, in 1485.

Eureka!
Archimedes, the Greek mathematician and inventor (287-212 B.C.) exclaimed "Eureka" when he discovered a method to test the purity of gold.

The moon is made of green cheese.
Englishman John Heywood (1497-1580) wrote this in his book *Dialogue on Wit and Folly.*

We hold these truths to be self-evident, that all men and women are created equal.
Suffragette Elizabeth Cady Stanton added the word "women" to this well-known line from the Declaration of Independence. The line was part of a speech she gave at the First Women's Rights Convention held in Seneca Falls, New York, on July 19, 1848.

CB RADIO SLANG

Truckers on the road use CB (Citizens Band) radios to talk to other truckers.

Bear	Policeman	**Pumpkin**	Flat tire
Cut some z's	Get some sleep	**Read**	Hear
Hole in the wall	Tunnel	**Roger**	Yes
Piggy bank	Toll booth	**Tar**	Coffee
Pit stop	Gas stop	**Ten-four**	Okay

WISE WORDS FROM *POOR RICHARD'S ALMANACK* BY BENJAMIN FRANKLIN

• If you do what you should not, you must hear what you would not.

• Don't thrown stones at your neighbors, if your own windows are glass.

• Some are weatherwise, some are otherwise.

• Lost time is never found again.

• Fish and visitors stink in three days.

SIX WAYS TO SIGN A LETTER OR AN AUTOGRAPH BOOK

Yours till the mail boxes
Yours till the bed spreads
Yours till the kitchen sinks
Yours till the board walks
Yours till Niagara Falls

Yours till elephants have suit cases instead of trucks

The Language of Numbers

NUMBERS ABOVE ONE MILLION

Name of Number	Number of Zeroes after 1	Name of Number	Number of Zeroes after
Million	6	Sextillion	21
Billion	9	Septillion	24
Trillion	12	Octillion	27
Quadrillion	15	Nonillion	30
Quintillion	18	Decillion	33

Name of Number	Number of Zeroes after 1	Name of Number	Number of Zeroes after
Undecillion	36	Sexdecillion	51
Duodecillion	39	Septendecillion	54
Tredecillin	42	Octodecillion	57
Quattuordecillion	45	Novemdecillion	60
Quindecellion	48	Centillion	303

ROMAN NUMERALS

Arabic	Roman	Arabic	Roman
1	I	40	XL
2	II	49	XLIX
3	III	50	L
4	IV	60	LX
5	V	80	LXXX
6	VI	90	XC
7	VII	99	XCIX
8	VIII	100	C
9	IX	101	CI
10	X	111	CXI
11	XI	200	CC
12	XII	400	CCCC
13	XIII	500	D
18	XVIII	600	DC
19	XIX	900	CM
20	XX	1000	M
21	XXI	1900	MCM
29	XXIX	1988	MCMLXXXVIII
30	XXX	2000	MM

MATHEMATICAL SHAPES

Name of Shape	Number of Sides	Name of Shape	Number of Sides
Quadrilateral	4	Octagon	8
Pentagon	5	Nonagon	9
Hexagon	6	Decagon	10
Heptagon	7	Dodecagon	12

MEASUREMENTS

Acre	4840 square yards	Land measurement
Baker's dozen	13	Number of objects
Bushel	4 pecks	Dry measurement
Carat	200 milligrams	Weight of precious stones
Fathom	6 feet	Measures depth of water
Foot	12 inches	Distance
Gross	12 dozen or 144	Number of objects
Hand	4 inches	Measures height of horses
Knot	1.151 survey miles	Speed over water
League	3 survey miles	Distance over land
Liter	1.057 liquid quarts	Liquid measurement
Marathon	26 miles, 385 yards	Distance of a foot race
Mile	1760 yards	Distance
Peck	8 quarts	Dry measurement
Score	20	Number of objects
Ton	short, 2000 pounds; long, 2240 pounds	Weight

Music

What do Reginald Dwight and George Alan O'Dowd have in common?
Answer: They're both famous rock 'n' roll stars! However, you know
them better as Elton John and Boy George. In this chapter, you'll find
out the original names of famous performers, plus facts on other kinds
of musicmakers, popular dances, greatest hits, music slang, and more.

Music Trivia

1. **What is the bestselling record of all time?**

   ANSWER: "White Christmas," the 1942 recording sung by Bing
   Crosby.

2. **Who was the youngest person to have a number-one single?**

   ANSWER: Stevie Wonder was 13 years old when his recording,
   "Fingertips," topped the charts.

3. **Who was the oldest person to have a number-one single?**

   ANSWER: Singer and trumpeter Louis Armstrong was 64 when
   "Hello Dolly" was number one.

4. How many copies of a record must be sold for it to be awarded a Gold Record? A Platinum Record?

    ANSWER: In the U.S., Gold Records are awarded to single records that sell one million copies. Platinum Records are awarded to those selling two million.

5. What was the first rock video aired on MTV?

    ANSWER: "Video Killed the Radio Star," by the Bugles, aired at midnight on August 1, 1981.

6. What song was sung on the moon and played on the air on Earth?

    ANSWER: "While Strolling Through the Park One Day."

7. What U.S. vice president wrote a number-one hit song?

    ANSWER: In the 1920s, Charles Gates Dawes, vice president to Calvin Coolidge and a Nobel Peace Prize winner, wrote "Melody in A Major." The tune was revived in 1958 for a pop song called "It's All in the Game," sung by Tommy Edwards.

8. What is the oldest music group in the U.S.?

    ANSWER: The United States Marine band was formed by Congress in 1798 and played for Thomas Jefferson's inauguration in 1801. From 32 drums and fifes, the band has grown to 140 members. It is known as "The President's Own."

9. What were the longest-lasting number-one rock 'n' roll singles?

    ANSWER: "Don't be Cruel" and "Hound Dog," sung by Elvis Presley, were both number one for 11 weeks in 1956.

10. Which hit song has been recorded by the most artists?

    ANSWER: The 1965 hit "Yesterday," by Beatles John Lennon and Paul McCartney. Between 1965 and 1973, 1,186 versions of this song were recorded.

11. Who were the first ten inductees into the Rock and Roll Hall of Fame?

    ANSWER: Chuck Berry, James Brown, Ray Charles, Sam Cooke, Fats Domino, the Everly Brothers, Buddy Holly, Jerry Lee Lewis, Elvis Presley, and Little Richard were inducted in 1986.

Music Slang

Axe—The general term for a musician's instrument.

Bones—A trombone.

Burn—To play with intensity, with "heat."

Cans—Headphones worn by recording musicians.

Clam—A wrong note, a mistake.

Dues—The sacrifices a musician makes before becoming successful; also known as "to pay your dues."

Gig—A job.

Gig bag—A soft-covered case for carrying a musical instrument.

Eighty-eights—A piano. A piano has eighty-eight keys.

Harp—A harmonica.

Hook—A catchy melodic phrase or lyric that is particularly memorable.

Ivories—Another term for piano. Piano keys are made of ivory.

Jamming—Making up music as you play it, just for the fun of it; improvisation.

Kick—A bass drum.

Lick—An extemporaneous musical flourish improvised by a musician.

Licorice stick—A clarinet.

Pipes—A singer's voice.

Tubs—Drums.

Wail—To play or sing with deep feeling.

Musical Notes

REAL NAMES OF FAMOUS MUSICIANS

Gary U.S. Bonds—Gary Anderson

Chubby Checker—Ernest Evans

John Denver—Henry John Deutschendorf, Jr.

Boy George—George Alan O'Dowd

Chaka Khan—Yvette Stevens

Elton John—Reginald Dwight

Madonna—Madonna Louise Veronica Ciccone

Prince—Prince Rogers Nelson

Stevie Wonder—Steveland Judkins Morris

BILLBOARD'S LIST OF TOP POP SINGLES

Year	Song	Performer
1986	"That's What Friends Are For"	Dionne Warwick & Friends
1985	"Careless Whisper"	Wham! (featuring George Michaels)
1984	"When Doves Cry"	Prince
1983	"Every Breath You Take"	Police
1982	"Physical"	Olivia Newton-John
1981	"Bette Davis Eyes"	Kim Carnes
1980	"Call Me"	Blondie
1979	"My Sharona"	Knack
1978	"Shadow Dancing"	Andy Gibb
1977	"Tonight's the Night (Gonna Be Alright)"	Rod Stewart
1976	"Silly Love Songs"	Wings

PRESIDENTIAL CAMPAIGN SONGS

President	Campaign Song	Campaign Year
Franklin Delano Roosevelt	"Happy Days Are Here Again"	1932
Harry S. Truman	"I'm Just Wild About Harry"	1948
John F. Kennedy	"High Hopes"	1960
James Earl Carter	"Why Not the Best"	1978

POPULAR SONGS FOR A CAUSE

"Ain't Gonna Play Sun City"—Against apartheid in South Africa.

"Ballad of Ira Hayes"—For the plight of the American Indian.

"Blowin' in the Wind"—Anti-war and civil rights song.

"Do They Know It's Christmas"—To make people aware of the problem of world hunger.

"I Ain't Marchin' Anymore"—Vietnam war protest song.

"Imagine"—An appeal for world peace and brotherhood.

"Save the Whales"—Against the slaughter of whales.

"We Are The World"—For famine victims in Ethiopia.

"We Shall Overcome"—For civil rights in the U.S.

FAMOUS ROCK CONCERTS FOR A CAUSE

AMNESTY INTERNATIONAL
A series of concerts to benefit this human-rights organization was held in six U.S. cities over a two-week period in 1986. The final concert was held at Giants Stadium in New Jersey on June 15, 1986. Amnesty International documents and tries to help people around the world who have been imprisoned by their governments.

BANGLADESH
Organized by ex-Beatle George Harrison, this concert was held in Madison Square Garden in New York City on August 1, 1971. The money from the concert and the concert record album went to help victims of war in Bangladesh.

CHERNOBYL
The first concert staged in the U.S.S.R. to raise money for a cause was held in Kiev, Russia, in May 1986. Soviet rock stars performed to raise money for the victims of the nuclear plant accident at Chernobyl earlier that year.

FARM AID
Fifty country and rock performers held a concert in Champaign, Illinois, on September 22, 1985, to help support the American farmer. The concert raised 10 million dollars and focused nationwide attention on the economic problems suffered by farmers.

LIVE-AID
A 16-hour concert, featuring some of the most popular rock stars in the world, was held in Philadelphia and London on July 13, 1985. It raised over 50 million dollars. The money went to help save the lives of famine victims in Ethiopia and the Sudan.

MUSICALLY GIFTED KIDS

The following nine performers got their start when they were kids.

LOUIS ARMSTRONG
Trumpeter/singer Louis Armstrong, known as "Satchmo," was one of the greatest jazz musicians of all time. He learned to play the trumpet when he was thirteen and started performing soon after.

ARETHA FRANKLIN
Known as "Lady Soul," Aretha Franklin made her first recording when she was fifteen years old. She started as a gospel singer but has become recognized as a blues, pop, and jazz singer.

?

JUDY GARLAND

Judy Garland, born Frances Gumm, appeared on the vaudeville stage with her sisters when she was three. By the time she was ten, her singing voice was "big and resonant" and thrilled live audiences. At the age of sixteen, she sang "Over the Rainbow" in the movie *The Wizard of Oz*. Her rendition of the song became a classic and established her as a popular singer.

BENNY GOODMAN

The great jazz clarinettist Benny Goodman began performing with his brothers before he was a teenager. At the age of thirteen, he became the youngest member of the musicians' union. Best known as a jazz musician, Goodman also recorded works by Mozart and Beethoven.

MICHAEL JACKSON

Singer/songwriter Michael Jackson began performing at the age of five with his brothers, The Jackson 5. On his own, he has recorded many hits and coauthored the song "We Are The World."

GLADYS KNIGHT

At the age of fourteen, Gladys Knight first performed with the "Pips." She began as a gospel singer and is now recognized as a great soul and pop singer.

PAUL MCCARTNEY

Former Beatle Paul McCartney wrote "Love Me Do" with John Lennon when he was fifteen. As a Beatle, solo performer, and songwriter, he has contributed greatly to popular music.

HANK WILLIAMS

Nicknamed the "Hillbilly Shakespeare," Hank Williams was a songwriter and singer of great appeal. He had his own string band at the age of thirteen and his own radio show soon after. He was one of the first three people elected to the Country Music Hall of Fame.

STEVIE WONDER

At the age of ten, Stevie Judkins was singing and playing the harmonica on a street corner in Detroit. At the age of thirteen, as "Little Stevie Wonder," he topped the charts with a hit single "Fingertips."

That's Dancing

DANCING AROUND THE WORLD

Country or Region of Origin	Dance	Country or Region of Origin	Dance
Argentina	Tango	Italy	Tarantella
Brazil	Samba	Middle European	Polka, Shottische
Caribbean Islands	Cha-cha	Scotland	Highland Fling, Jig
Cuba	Conga, Mambo, Rumba	Spain	Bolero, Fandango, Flamenco
England	Hornpipe, Morris Dance	U.S.	Charleston, Fox-Trot, Jitterbug, Lindy Hop, Square Dances
France	Cancan, Minuet		
Germany	Waltz		
Ireland	Fading, Jig		
Israel	Hora		

FAMOUS ROCK 'N' ROLL DANCES

Break Dancing	Monkey	Hitchhiker	Stroll
Bugaloo	Pony	Hully Gully	Swim
Fish	Shake	Jerk	Twist
Frug	Slam Dancing	Mashed Potatoes	Watusi

?

People

All kinds of people are featured in this chapter. Some have become legends; others have become part of our language. You'll read about kids who made history, Oscar-winning kids, families of fame, and more in this celebrity roundup.

Historical People

FIVE YOUNG KINGS

TUTANKHAMEN—RULER OF ANCIENT EGYPT, CIRCA 1358 B.C.
Tutankhamen became Pharoah (king) of Egypt when he was about eight or nine and ruled until his death nine years later. King "Tut" is remembered more for his tomb than for his reign. In 1922, the unopened tomb was discovered with its four rooms of treasures and a coffin of solid gold. The treasures of "Tut" have been shown in museums throughout the world.

EDWARD V—KING OF ENGLAND, 1483

At the age of thirteen, Edward V became king. Within a short time, his uncle, Richard, Duke of Gloucester, imprisoned Edward, along with his younger brother, in the Tower of London and took over the throne.

The young king and his brother disappeared, and to this day, no one knows exactly what happened to them. It is widely believed that the boys were smothered to death in their sleep by order of Richard. However, some sources suggest that Henry VII, the king after Richard, had the boys killed.

EDWARD VI—KING OF ENGLAND, 1547-1553

Edward VI was the son of King Henry VIII and his third wife, Jane Seymour. Edward VI became king at the age of ten when his father died. He reigned for six years under the control of his uncle, Edward Seymour. He is remembered for founding English grammar schools. Edward VI died at the age of sixteen from tuberculosis.

FRANCIS II—KING OF FRANCE, 1559-1560

Fifteen-year-old Francis became king when his father, Henry II, died of a head wound sustained in a lancing bout in a tournament. The death of his father had been predicted by famous psychic Nostradamus four years earlier. Francis II died at age sixteen, having reigned for less than eight months.

PETER I—RULER OF RUSSIA, 1682-1725

At age ten, Peter ruled Russia with his half brother, Ivan. When he was seventeen, he assumed full power. Known as Peter the Great, he is most remembered for Westernizing Russia.

KIDS WHO MADE HISTORY

GRACE BEDELL

Abraham Lincoln was the first U.S. president to wear a beard. He did so at the suggestion of eleven-year-old Grace Bedell of Westfield, New York. She sent him a letter saying "You would look a great deal better, for your face is so thin. All the ladies like whiskers and they would tease their husbands to vote for you and then you would be president." Soon after receiving the letter, Lincoln did grow a beard. Later, when he met Grace, he kissed her and said "You see, I let the whiskers grow for you, Grace."

?

BENNY BENSON

Thirteen-year-old Benny Benson of Seward, Alaska, made history when he designed the official Alaskan state flag. When Alaska was still a territory (it became a state in 1959), a contest was held among 7th- to 12th-grade Alaskan students to design a flag. Benny's design—simple, original, and symbolic—won. In 1927, it became the official flag of Alaska.

LINDA BROWN

This young black schoolgirl living in Topeka, Kansas, in the 1950s, had to travel more than two miles to go to a black elementary school, even though there was a white school four blocks from her home. Her parents sued the school district for its policy of school segregation. In 1954, the U.S. Supreme Court directed schools to open their classrooms to *all* children in the *Brown* vs. *Board of Education* decision. Linda Brown played an important part in that change in American education.

BOBBY FISCHER

Bobby Fischer was born in Chicago, Illinois. He grew up in Brooklyn, New York, where at the age of six he was taught to play chess by his older sister. In 1958, when he was just fifteen, he earned the title of International Grand Master. He was the youngest person in the world to win that title. Bobby Fischer went on to become the world chess champion, holding that title from 1972 to 1975.

ANNE FRANK

From 1942 to 1944, Jewish teenager Anne Frank kept a secret diary while she and her family were forced into hiding from the Nazis. When her family was finally discovered, they were sent to concentration camps, where only her father survived. The women who had hidden the Franks found the diary and gave it to Anne's father after he was released. It was published in 1947 as *The Diary of Anne Frank* and has since served as an example of human courage and as a reminder of the horrors of the Holocaust.

SYBIL LUDINGTON

In 1777, during the Revolutionary War, an exhausted army messenger arrived at the home of the Ludingtons in Connecticut. He was unable to ride any further, so sixteen-year-old Sybil Ludington finished the messenger's mission: to get needed reinforcements for the American Army. She rode her horse for 40 miles at night to get the help that drove the British back to their ships. A statue of Sybil on horseback stands in Carmel, New York, today.

SAMANTHA SMITH

When Samantha Smith of Maine was eleven years old, she wrote a letter to the leader of Russia, then Yuri Andropov. Her letter was a plea to stop the nuclear arms race. Mr. Andropov responded by asking her to visit him at the Kremlin. Samantha made history when she and her parents traveled to Russia to meet with the Russian premier in 1983. The whole world mourned when Samantha Smith died in an airplane crash in 1985.

PEOPLE WHO BECAME LEGENDS

BEAU BRUMMELL

George Bryan Brummell was an English dandy (overly stylish dresser) who lived from 1778 to 1840. His keen interest in dress and fashion influenced the men of his day to wear dark, simply cut clothes and trousers rather than breeches (short pants reaching just below the knee). He was so concerned with his own dress he would often wear three different outfits in one day. His boots were polished like mirrors and his collars were starched so stiffly that he could not turn his head. Today, a fashion-conscious man is sometimes called a "Beau Brummell."

CALAMITY JANE

Martha Jane Canary was an American frontierswoman who lived from 1852 to 1903. A famous and deadly shot, she dressed in men's clothing and drifted throughout the Southwest bragging about her exploits as an Indian fighter and army scout. Later, she toured in a traveling burlesque show.

CASANOVA
Giovanni Jacopo Casanova de Seingalt lived in Italy in the 18th century. He traveled throughout Europe as a gambler, spy, and "ladies man." Today, an overly amorous male is often called a "casanova."

CASEY JONES
John Luther Jones, an American locomotive engineer, was nicknamed Casey because he worked in Cayce, Kentucky. On April 29, 1900, he was driving the Cannon Ball Express from Memphis, Tennessee, to Canton, Mississippi, when his train came upon a stalled freight train on the track in front of him. Casey managed to stop his train and save the lives of the passengers, but he was killed in the accident. From that day on, he has been remembered as a hero in song and story.

ST. NICHOLAS
The Bishop of Myra, who lived in Asia Minor during the 4th century A.D., is thought to be the famous St. Nicholas. Because of his fondness for children, he is remembered as their patron saint. The early English settlers in New York adopted him from the Dutch settlers and called him Santa Claus.

ST. PATRICK
This Christian missionary lived from A.D. 385 to 461. The real story of his life is confused by the many legends associated with him. It is said that he was born in Britain and enslaved by the Irish. After some time, he escaped to Gaul (ancient France). He later returned to Ireland to convert the Irish people to Christianity. By the time of his death, Ireland was Christianized.

Remarkable Relatives

FAMOUS "MOTHERS"

MOTHER HALE
Clara Hale of New York City has raised forty foster children and cared for more than five hundred babies of drug-addicted mothers. In 1985,

President Ronald Reagan cited her as "a true American hero." She cares for the children at Hale House, which is located in central Harlem in New York City. Clara Hale was born in 1905 in Philadelphia, Pennsylvania.

MOTHER JONES
Mary Harris Jones spent most of her lifetime crusading against low wages and poor working conditions for children, coal miners, and railroad workers in the U.S. She was born in Ireland in 1830 and died in the U.S. in 1930.

MOTHER SETON
Elizabeth Ann Seton was a teacher and Roman Catholic religious leader who founded an order of sisters, the Daughters of Charity. She also helped establish the parochial school system in the U.S. She was born in New York in 1774 and died in 1821. In 1975, she was canonized as the first American-born saint.

MOTHER TERESA
Agnes Bojaxhiu was born in Yugoslavia in 1910. At age eighteen, she became a nun and served as a teacher in Calcutta, India for twenty years. She left her convent to work for the poor and sick people in the slums of Calcutta. She founded the Missionaries of Charity and was awarded a Nobel Peace Prize for her work in 1979.

WHISTLER'S MOTHER
When James Whistler painted a portrait of his mother, Anna McNeill Whistler, he captured a woman of patience and created a symbol of motherhood. Her image is so popular that it is found on greeting cards, posters, playing cards, and T-shirts. In 1934, the United States issued a three-cent postage stamp with a picture of Mrs. Whistler "in memory and honor of the Mothers of America."

The title of the painting, in which Anna Whistler is shown seated in a chair, is "Arrangement in Black and Gray No. 1, The Artist's Mother."

FAMOUS "FATHERS"

"Father of His Country"	George Washington (1732-1799), the first president of the United States.
"Father of History"	Herodotus (c. 484-c. 425 B.C.), Greek historian, the first to write a history of Western civilization.
"Father of India"	Mohandas "Mahatma" Gandhi (1869-1948), Indian leader of nationalist movement against British rule.
"Father of Medicine"	Hippocrates (c. 460-c. 377 B.C.), Greek doctor who was the first to define medicine as a science.
"Father of Science Fiction"	Jules Verne (1828-1905), French novelist and the originator of modern science fiction.
"Father of the Skyscraper"	Cass Gilbert (1859-1934), U.S. architect who designed the tallest building of his era, the Woolworth Building in New York City.
"Father of the Symphony"	Franz Joseph Haydn (1732-1809), Austrian composer whose symphonic forms inspired such composers as Mozart and Beethoven. His best-known symphonies are probably the Surprise Symphony and the Clock Symphony.

FAMOUS BROTHERS

THE MARX BROTHERS

This famous comedy team of stage and screen featured five brothers:

Arthur (1888-1964)—Mime and harp player, known as "Harpo."

Herbert (1901-1979)—Known as "Zeppo."

Julius (1890-1977)—Master of the one-line joke, known as "Groucho."

Leonard (1887-1961)—The piano player, known as "Chico."

Milton (1897-1977)—Known as "Gummo," he eventually became the Marx Brothers' manager.

THE MAYO BROTHERS
These two brothers were surgeons and co-founders of the internationally-known Mayo Clinic in Rochester, Minnesota.

William (1861-1939)—Specialized in abdominal surgery.

Charles (1865-1939)—Specialized in goiter and cataract operations.

THE KENNEDY BROTHERS
Three brothers active in U.S. government and politics:

John F. (1917-1963)—U.S. president, 1961 to 1963. Assassinated in 1963.

Robert F. (1925-1968)—U.S. Attorney General, U.S. Senator from New York and presidential candidate. Assassinated in 1968.

Edward M. (1932-)—U.S. Senator from Massachusetts.

THE WRIGHT BROTHERS
These two brothers worked together as airplane inventors and made history when they became the first to fly a power-driven airplane:

Orville (1871-1948)—He won the toss of a coin and was the first to fly their plane, "The Flyer," on December 17, 1903.

Wilbur (1867-1912)—He made the fourth flight that day. It lasted 59 seconds.

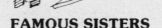

FAMOUS SISTERS

BRONTE SISTERS
Three sisters who were English novelists and poets:

Charlotte (1816-1855)—Her best-known novel is *Jane Eyre*.

Emily (1818-1848)—Her single great novel is *Wuthering Heights*.

Anne (1820-1849)—Her first and best-known novel is *Agnes Grey*.

ANN LANDERS AND ABIGAIL VAN BUREN
Twin sisters Esther Friedman (Ann) and Pauline Friedman (Abigail) are journalists and advice columnists:

?

Ann Landers (1918-)—She writes the "Ann Landers" column. United Press International once voted her among the 10 most important women in the U.S.

Abigail Van Buren (1918-)—Her "Dear Abby" column is syndicated in over eight hundred newspapers throughout the world.

The Name Game

Ten People Whose Names Became Words

CHARLES BOYCOTT

Boycott: To refuse to have dealings with in protest. Charles Boycott was an English landlord living in Ireland in the late 1800s. He forced many people out of their homes by raising their rents. In turn, the people banded together and stopped his mail, cut off his food and supplies, and forced his servants to leave.

NICHOLAS CHAUVIN

Chauvinism: Fanatical devotion to a country or group. Nicholas Chauvin was a soldier who fought for Napoleon. His blind faith in his leader, even after Napoleon's exile, was ridiculed by his fellow soldiers.

DERICK

Derrick: A hoisting apparatus that uses a tackle rigged to a rope or cable. Derick was a 17th-century English hangman at the Tyburn Prison in London. The gallows in the prison resemble the hoisting machine known as a derrick.

JOHN DUNS SCOTUS

Dunce: A stupid or dull-witted person. John Duns Scotus was a philosopher and teacher who lived in Scotland in the 13th century. Those who opposed his teachings called his followers "Dunces."

DR. JOSEPH GUILLOTIN

Guillotine: A machine for beheading by means of a heavy blade that falls between two guides. Dr. Joseph Guillotin was a French physician who did not invent this beheading machine but proposed its use as a humanitarian way of putting criminals to death. As a result, in 1792, the guillotine became the instrument of execution in France.

PATRICK HOOLIGAN

Hooligan: A hoodlum or young roughneck. Patrick Hooligan was a brawling boisterous Irishman who lived in London in the late 1800s.

KING MAUSOLUS

Mausoleum: A large tomb, usually a stone building. King Mausolus ruled Caria (now part of Turkey) in the 4th century B.C. When he died, his wife had a huge burial monument built for him at Halicarnassus. It is considered one of the Seven Wonders of the Ancient World.

SAMUEL MAVERICK

Maverick: An unbranded range animal; also an individual who doesn't go along with the group. Samuel Maverick was a pioneer who lived in Texas in the 1800s. He owned a herd of cattle that he left unbranded. His neighbors began to call all unbranded stray cattle mavericks.

AMBROSE BURNSIDE

Sideburns: Side whiskers, a continuation of the hairline in front of the ears. Ambrose Burnside was an American general and politician who lived in the 1800s. He was often in the public eye and those who copied his growth of whiskers at the side of his face called them "burnsides." Eventually, "burnsides" was changed to "sideburns," an anagram (rearrangement of letters) for his name.

THEODORE ROOSEVELT

Teddy bear: A stuffed toy bear. When President Theodore (Teddy) Roosevelt refused to shoot a stray bear cub while on a hunting trip, the story was told in all the newspapers of the day. After seeing a cartoon of the event, toymakers began making soft, lovable "teddy bears."

Names Behind Initials

Initials	Name	Occupation
P.T. Barnum	Phineas Taylor	U.S. showman, circus owner
e.e. cummings	Edward Estlin	U.S. poet
W.E.B. Dubois	William Edward Burghardt	U.S. civil rights leader
T.S. Eliot	Thomas Stearns	British poet, playwright
W.C. Fields	William Claude	U.S. comic, film actor
A.J. Foyt	Anthony Joseph	U.S. race car driver
I.M. Pei	Ieoh Ming	U.S. architect
J.C. Penny	James Cash	U.S. merchant
J.D. Salinger	Jerome David	U.S. author
E.W. Scripps	Edward Wyllis	U.S. newspaper publisher
O.J. Simpson	Orenthal James	U.S. football player
Y.A. Tittle	Yelberton Abraham	U.S. football player
J.M.W. Turner	Joseph Mallord William	British painter
J.R.R. Tolkein	John Ronald Reuel	British author
H.G. Wells	Herbert George	British author

Five U.S. Cities Named After People

Cleveland, Ohio	Named after General Moses Cleaveland, who laid out the city in 1796.
Dallas, Texas	Named after George Dallas, a friend of the city's first settler, John Bryan. Dallas later became U.S. vice-president under James Polk.
Denver, Colorado	Named after James Denver, governor of the Kansas Territory of which eastern Colorado was a part.

Houston, Texas	Named after Samuel Houston, a hero of the Texas war for independence from Mexico.
Orlando, Florida	Originally named after its first settler, Aaron Jernigan, in 1857, Orlando was renamed after Orlando Reeves, a soldier who died in a fight with local Indians.

NICKNAMES

Nicknames Of Famous People

Nickname	*Real Name*	*Origin*
Buffalo Bill	William Frederick Cody	Cody earned this nickname for his exploits as a buffalo hunter as well as a U.S. Army scout.
Molly Pitcher	Mary McCauley	This American Revolutionary War heroine carried water to thirsty soldiers at the Battle of Monmouth.
Zero Mostel	Sam Mostel	This U.S. actor was given the nickname in school for his zero marks.
Ringo Starr	Richard Starkey	The drummer for the Beatles, he was called "Ringo" because he liked to wear lots of rings.
Twiggy	Lesley Hornby	An English model of the 1960s, Twiggy earned her nickname because of her tall, thin body.

Nicknames of Kings & Queens

"Bloody Mary" — Mary I, Queen of England (1553-1558), earned her nickname because of her religious persecution of Protestants.

"Ivan the Terrible" — Ivan IV, Russian ruler from 1547 to 1584, was called "the Terrible" because of his reign of terror and fits of fury. He killed his son, Ivan, in a rage and disposed of seven wives.

"Louis the Fat" — Louis VI was king of France from 1108 to 1137. In his forties, he gained so much weight that he could not mount his horse.

OTHER LOUIS:

Louis II—"the Stammerer"
Louis V—"the Sluggard"
Louis VII—"the Young"
Louis X—"the Quarrelsome"
Louis XI—"the Cruel"

"Peter the Mad" — Peter III, ruler of Russia (1761-1762), earned his nickname because of his many temper tantrums. He was also said to be mentally unbalanced.

"Silly Billy" — William IV, king of Great Britain from 1830 to 1837, was dubbed "Silly Billy" because of his eccentric behavior.

Academy Award-Winning Kids

The young performers below were given special Oscars for their contributions to film.

Name	Age	Year	Name	Age	Year
Shirley Temple	6	1934	**Judy Garland**	17	1939
Mickey Rooney	18	1938	**Margaret O'Brian**	7	1944
Deanna Durbin	16	1938	**Tatum O'Neal**	10	1973*

*O'Neal is the only young person to have won a supporting actress Oscar. She received one for her role as Addie in the 1973 movie, *Paper Moon*.

Heroes of Young America: A Poll*

CONDUCTED BY THE EDITORS OF *THE WORLD ALMANAC AND BOOK OF FACTS®*

1980 Burt Reynolds, actor

1981 Burt Reynolds, actor

1982 Alan Alda, TV and movie actor.

1983 Sylvester Stallone, actor, director, and writer

1984 Michael Jackson, pop singer

1985 Eddie Murphy, comic actor

1986 Bill Cosby, comedian, actor

*Voted by 7th-12th graders throughout the U.S.

Legendary "Little People"

Creatures of Folklore and Fairy Tales

Brownies These small creatures are said to be friendly and helpful. Legend has it that they live in homes with real people. At night, while the family sleeps, brownies do household chores.

Elves These mischievous fairies are often unpleasant. It is said they are little people without souls.

Gnomes These small people are often deformed and never age. They live in the earth—often in mines—where they guard precious ores or treasure.

Goblins Ugly and often mean, goblins like to live in dark places. They often inhabit people's homes.

Gremlins These bad-tempered creatures are said to cause malfunctions of aircraft equipment.

Leprechauns Leprechauns are said to be very rich and very stingy. They hoard pots of gold and will reveal the hiding places of the gold only if they are caught by humans.

Trolls Trolls may be either very small or very large. They live either in caves, by the sea, or in mountains.

Places to Visit in the U.S.A.

Would you like to see a castle made of corn, or a "palace" dedicated to the King of Rock 'n' Roll? How about a parade, or a museum where you can dig for dinosaur fossils? This chapter is filled with fun places for kids to visit, including national parks, theme parks, and sports halls of fame.

Parks

THEME PARKS

DOGPATCH
Harrison, Arkansas
The park features actors dressed as the characters in the *Li'l Abner* comic strip. There are rides as well as musical and animal shows to enjoy.

DOLLYWOOD
Pigeon Forge, Tennessee
An 1880s historical park named for the popular singer, Dolly Parton. There are rides, mountain crafts, music performances, and a Dolly Parton Museum.

HERSHEYPARK
Hershey, Pennsylvania
Rides, a dolphin show, and arts and craft displays can be enjoyed here, along with a kissing tower featuring chocolate kiss-shaped windows. Visitors can also tour the Hershey Chocolate World right next door.

OLD STURBRIDGE VILLAGE
Sturbridge, Massachusetts
Visitors can see what life was like in rural New England between 1790 and 1830. There are homes, shops, and mills to visit with a staff of people dressed in historical costumes.

OLD TUCSON
Tucson, Arizona
The Old West is the theme of this park and movie studio. Live gunfights and horseback and stagecoach rides along desert trails are also part of the fun.

SANTA'S VILLAGE
Skyforest, California
Santa, along with his reindeer, can be visited in this park. There are also rides, such as the Whirling Christmas Tree.

SPACE WORLD
Detroit, Michigan
Attractions including what it would be like to walk on the moon and travel at the speed of light are featured here. There are also exhibits on space technology and life in the future.

THE FIVE MOST POPULAR
NATIONAL PARKS IN THE U.S.A.
(LISTED IN ORDER OF NUMBER OF VISITORS THEY ATTRACT)

1. **Great Smoky Mountain National Park**, North Carolina and Tennessee. The lovely mountain scenery of the Smoky Mountains along with early pioneer log cabins, barns, and farm implements can be seen here. The park is 520,269 acres.

2. **Acadia National Park**, Maine. Visitors can see the rugged Maine coastline with high cliffs and sandy beaches. Cadillac Mountain, 1,530 feet high, is in this park. The park is 39,707 acres.

3. **Rocky Mountain National Park**, Colorado. An outstanding view

of more than 107 mountain peaks over 11,000 feet high is part of this 265,193-acre park. The park abounds with wildlife and flowers.

4. **Grand Teton National Park**, Wyoming. There are spectacular views of the Teton Mountain range here. Jackson Hole, a winter feeding ground for elk, is in this 310,528-acre park.

5. **Olympic National Park**, Washington. Glaciers, lakes, rain forests, and some 50 miles of coastline attract visitors from all over the world. This 914,576-acre park is located in the highest part of the coast ranges and features Mt. Olympus.

Sports Halls Of Fame

Below is a list of the location of the halls of fame for various sports.

AUTO RACING
Auto Racing Hall of Fame
4700 West 16th Street
Speedway, Indiana 46224

BOWLING
**National Bowling Hall of Fame
and Museum**
5301 South 76th Street
Greendale, Wisconsin 53129

BASEBALL
**National Baseball Hall of Fame
and Museum**
Cooperstown, New York 13326

FISHING
**National Fresh Water Fishing
Hall of Fame**
Wisconsin Avenue
Hayward, Wisconsin 54843

BASKETBALL
**Naismith Memorial
Basketball Hall of Fame**
460 Alden Street
Springfield, Massachusetts 01109

FOOTBALL
**Professional Football Hall of
Fame**
2121 Harrison Avenue, N.W.
Canton, Ohio 44708

Canadian Football Hall of Fame
58 Jackson Street West
Hamilton, Ontario, Canada

GOLF
World Golf Hall of Fame
Box 908
Pinehurst, North Carolina 28374

HOCKEY
NHL
Exhibition Place
Toronto, Ontario, Canada

Hockey Hall of Fame
Hat Trick Avenue
Eveleth, Minnesota 55734

LACROSSE
Lacrosse Hall of Fame and Museum
Newton H. White, Jr. Athletic Center
Baltimore, Maryland 21218

RODEO
Professional Rodeo Hall of Champions
Colorado Springs, Colorado 80901

SAILING
Sailing Hall of Fame
U.S. Naval Academy
Annapolis, Maryland 21402

SKATING
Speed Skating Hall of Fame
Recreation Center
Newburgh, New York 12550

SKIING
National Ski Hall of Fame
P.O. Box 191
Ishpeming, Michigan 49849

SOFTBALL
National Softball Hall of Fame
2810 Northeast 50th Street
Oklahoma City, Oklahoma 73125

SWIMMING
National Swimming Hall of Fame
One Hall of Fame Drive
Fort Lauderdale, Florida 33316

TRACK & FIELD
Track & Field Hall of Fame of the United States of America
1524 Kanaha Boulevard
Charleston, West Virginia 25311

United States Track & Field Hall of Fame
P.O. Box 297
Angola, Indiana 46703

WRESTLING
National Wrestling Hall of Fame
405 W. Hall of Fame Avenue
Stillwater, Oklahoma 74074

U.S. Parades

Parade	Month	City
Cherry Blossom	April (first week)	Washington, D.C.
Columbus Day	October 12th	New York, New York
Cotton Bowl	January 1st	Dallas, Texas
Macy's Thanksgiving Day	November	New York, New York
Mardi Gras	February	New Orleans, Louisiana
Mummers	January 1st	Philadelphia, Pennsylvania
Orange Bowl	January 1st	Miami, Florida
Pulaski Day	October 11th	New York, New York
St. Patrick's Day	March 17th	New York, New York
Thanksgiving Day	November	Philadelphia, Pennsylvania
Tournament of Roses	January 1st	Pasadena, California

Three Other Fun Places to Visit

THE CORN PALACE
Mitchell, South Dakota
This castle, decorated with thousands of ears of corn and prairie grass, was built in 1892. Every summer, the theme of the decorations is changed. The corn palace is also known as the "world's largest bird feeder" because it provides food for the canyon wren, a local bird.

GRACELAND
3764 Elvis Presley Boulevard
Memphis, Tennessee
The "palace" of the late Elvis Presley, known as the "King of Rock 'n' Roll," was opened to the public in 1982. The "king's" clothing, jewels, guitars, and other memorabilia are on display.

DISCOVERY DINOSAURS EXHIBIT
Philadelphia Academy of Natural Sciences
19th Street and Benjamin Franklin Parkway
Philadelphia, Pennsylvania
The Discovery Dinosaurs exhibit is one of the newest and most exciting exhibits of its kind. Life-size dinosaurs are depicted in a replica of a 70-million-year-old forest. Kids can dig for fossils, sit in giant dinosaur footprints, and assemble a dinosaur leg.

Presidents

Everyone is fascinated by the lives of the people who have been president of the United States. Here, for your enjoyment, is a treasury of hard-to-find facts about the presidents. You can liven up your school reports with facts about the following: favorite foods, family pets, first ladies, family life, and the White House.

Presidential Nicknames

President and Years in Office	Nickname and Reason
George Washington 1793-1793 1793-1797	**"Father of His Country"** He was the first president and commander in chief during the American Revolutionary War.
John Adams 1797-1801	**"Colossus of Debate"** He spoke out strongly against domination by the British.

President and Years in Office	Nickname and Reason
Thomas Jefferson 1801-1805 1805-1809	**"Man of the People"** He wrote the Declaration of Independence. While president, he stripped the office of its royal trappings, introduced the presidential handshake, and renamed the Presidential Palace the Executive Mansion.
James Madison 1809-1813 1813-1817	**"Father of the Constitution"** He was a principal contributor to the U.S. Constitution.
James Monroe 1817-1821 1821-1825	**"Last of the Cocked Hat"** He was the last of the generation of presidents involved in the American Revolution. Cocked hats were popular headgear of that era.
John Quincy Adams 1825-1829	**"Old Man Eloquent"** He was an exceptional public speaker.
Andrew Jackson 1829-1833 1833-1837	**"Old Hickory"** He was thought to be as tough and hard as hickory wood.
Martin van Buren 1837-1841	**"The Little Magician"** A clever politician, he was able to get what he wanted.
William Henry Harrison 1841	**"Old Tippecanoe"** While governor of Indiana, he led his army to victory over the Shawnee Indians in the Battle of Tippecanoe, 1811.
John Tyler 1841-1845	**"Accidental President"** He was the first vice-president to become president after the death of a president.
James Knox Polk 1845-1849	**"The Dark Horse"** When he was elected, many Americans did not know who he was.

?

President and Years in Office	Nickname and Reason
Zachary Taylor 1849-1850	**"Old Rough and Ready"** As a commanding soldier, he was always prepared for battle.
Millard Fillmore 1850-1853	**"His Accidency"** He became president as a result of the death of Zachary Taylor.
Franklin Pierce 1853-1857	**"Handsome Frank"** He was known for his good looks.
James Buchanan 1857-1861	**"Old Brick"** He was sixty-five years old when elected.
Abraham Lincoln 1861-1865	**"Honest Abe"** He had a lifelong reputation for honesty.
Andrew Johnson 1865-1869	**"The Tennessee Tailor"** He had humble beginnings as an uneducated tailor. (His wife taught him to read and write.)
Ulysses S. Grant 1869-1873 1873-1877	**"United States"** His first two initials were U.S.
Rutherford B. Hayes 1877-1881	**"Fraud President"** His opponent won the majority of popular votes, but he won the most electoral votes.
James A. Garfield 1881	**"Canal Boy"** As a youth he worked as a boatman on the Erie Canal.
Chester A. Arthur 1881-1885	**"Dude President"** He was always elegantly dressed.
Grover Cleveland 1885-1889 1893-1897	**"Uncle Jumbo"** He was a large, good-humored man.
Benjamin Harrison 1889-1893	**"Grandfather's Hat"** He was the grandson of former President William Henry Harrison.

President and Years in Office	Nickname and Reason
William McKinley 1897-1901	**"Napoleon of Protection"** He resembled Napoleon in looks and temperament. He was also a strong advocate of a protective tariff for the U.S.
Theodore Roosevelt 1901-1905 1905-1909	**"Rough Rider"** He commanded the fearless rough riders, a regiment of soldiers that fought in Cuba during the Spanish-American War.
William Taft 1909-1913	**"Big Bill"** He was a large man, weighing about 325 pounds.
Woodrow Wilson 1913-1917 1917-1921	**"The Professor"** He had a great intellect and was very well educated.
Calvin Coolidge 1923-1925 1925-1929	**"Silent Cal"** He was a shy man who spoke little.
Herbert Hoover 1929-1933	**"Grand Old Man"** He was an honored humanitarian.
Franklin Delano Roosevelt 1933-1937 1937-1941 1941-1945	**"F.D.R."** He was affectionately referred to by his initials.
Harry Truman 1945-1949 1949-1953	**"Give 'Em Hell Harry"** He spoke in a direct and candid manner.
Dwight D. Eisenhower 1953-1957 1957-1961	**"Ike"** A childhood nickname.
John Fitzgerald Kennedy 1961-1963	**"J.F.K."** He was often referred to by his initials.

President and Years in Office	Nickname and Reason
Lyndon Baines Johnson 1963-1965 1965-1969	**"L.B.J."** He was often referred to by his initials.
Richard M. Nixon 1969-1973 1973-1974	**"Tricky Dick"** He was first given this nickname in the 1950s because of his questionable political behavior. The term was revived when he became president.
Gerald Ford 1974-1977	**"Jerry"** Nickname for Gerald.
James Earl Carter 1977-1981	**"Jimmy"** Nickname for James. Carter preferred it to his more formal given name.
Ronald Reagan 1981-1985 1985-	**"The Great Communicator"** He was thought to be able to communicate well with people.

Favorite Foods of the Presidents

President	Foods
George Washington	Fish, onions, hazelnuts, tea.
John Adams	Codfish cakes, corn, gingerbread, hard cider.
Thomas Jefferson	Crabs, macaroni, olives, figs, fresh vegetables.
James Madison	Ice cream.
James Monroe	Chicken, breads and biscuits.
John Quincy Adams	Corn, fresh fruits.

President	Foods
Andrew Jackson	Wild turkey, partridge, venison, cheese, blackberries, milk.
Martin van Buren	Oysters, doughnuts, raisins, figs, apples.
William Henry Harrison	Beefsteak, eggnog, hard cider.
John Tyler	Oysters, quail, puddings.
James K. Polk	Ham, cornbread, fruitcake.
Zachary Taylor	Gumbo, okra, cherries.
Millard Fillmore	Meat, potatoes, cheese.
Franklin Pierce	Potatoes, fried apple pie.
James Buchanan	Lobster, chicken salad, grapes, almond-flavored sweets.
Abraham Lincoln	Beefsteak, corncakes, apples, pecan pie, coffee.
Andrew Johnson	Duck, wild turkey, fish, sweet potatoes, butter, milk.
Ulysses S. Grant	Roast beef, hominy grits, rice pudding, fried apples.
Rutherford B. Hayes	Eggs, cornmeal pancakes, apples.
James A. Garfield	Meat, potatoes, apple pie, tea.
Chester A. Arthur	Lamb chops, seafood, potatoes, fruit.
Grover Cleveland	Corned beef and cabbage, brown bread.
Benjamin Harrison	Soups, corn, figs.
William McKinley	Corned beef hash, lobster salad, eggs.
Theodore Roosevelt	Liver and bacon, kidney stew, wild greens, home-baked bread, mint-flavored foods, coffee, tea.
William Taft	Steak, seafoods, turtle soup, waffles, almonds.
Woodrow Wilson	Ham and eggs, biscuits, strawberry ice cream, white cake, butter, buttermilk.

President	Foods
Warren G. Harding	Chicken pot pie, knockwurst with sauerkraut.
Calvin Coolidge	Hot cereal, chicken, cornmeal biscuits, crackers with jam, pickles, maple syrup, porkapple pie.
Herbert Hoover	Lobster, carrot pudding, black cherries, homemade candy.
Franklin Delano Roosevelt	Creamed chipped beef, pepper pot soup, bread puddings, fried cornmeal mush, doughnuts.
Harry S. Truman	Brownies.
Dwight D. Eisenhower	Soups, beef stew, succotash, prune whip.
John F. Kennedy	Cinnamon toast, milk.
Richard M. Nixon	Cottage cheese, avocado salad.
Gerald Ford	Pot roast dinner, cottage cheese with A-1 Sauce, butter, pecan ice cream.
Jimmy Carter	Buttermilk, mixed nuts, licorice, peach ice cream.
Ronald Reagan	Macaroni and cheese, jelly beans.

Notable First Ladies

ABIGAIL SMITH ADAMS (1744-1818)
Abigail Adams, the wife of the second president, John Adams, is remembered for her strong views on women's rights. Long before they were accepted ideas, Abigail spoke out for women's right to vote and women's right to equal education. Abigail Adams was the only first lady to have a son who became president: John Quincy Adams, the sixth president of the U.S.

DOROTHEA PAYNE MADISON (1768-1849)

One of the most popular first ladies, "Dolley" Madison was the wife of the fourth president, James Madison. She was a very lively and gracious White House hostess. She was responsible for starting the traditional Easter egg roll for kids. During the War of 1812, Dolley Madison bravely stayed in the White House to make sure that important papers and other treasures were removed before the advancing British troops burned the house in 1814.

JULIA GARDINER TYLER (1820-1889)

Julia, the wife of the tenth president, John Tyler, was the first president's wife to have her portrait hung in the White House. On a return visit to the White House during Andrew Johnson's presidency, she convinced him to hang her portrait with those of the presidents, thus starting the tradition of first lady portraits. A young and fun-loving first lady, Julia Tyler was also the first to introduce dancing at White House receptions.

LUCY WARE WEBB HAYES (1831-1889)

Lucy, the wife of 19th president Rutherford Hayes, was the first president's wife to be called the first lady. A newspaper columnist used the term in describing her at her husband's inauguration. She was also the first president's wife to graduate from college. Well known for her charity work, she spent a great deal of time as first lady visiting schools, prisons, and mental institutions. An exceptional woman, Lucy was praised in poems by American poets Henry Wadsworth Longfellow and Oliver Wendell Holmes.

FRANCES FOLSOM CLEVELAND (1864-1947)

Frances was twenty-one years old when she became the first lady. She was the youngest first lady and the first wife of a president to give birth to a baby (Esther) in the White House. Frances was the wife of the 22nd president, Grover Cleveland.

HELEN HERRON TAFT (1861-1943)

Helen Taft, wife of William Taft, the 27th president, is best remembered for having three thousand cherry trees planted in Washington, D.C. The now famous trees of the nation's capital were a gift to her from the mayor of Tokyo, Japan.

ANNA ELEANOR ROOSEVELT (1884-1962)
Eleanor Roosevelt, wife of Franklin D. Roosevelt, the 32nd president, was one of the most active and influential first ladies. She wrote a daily newspaper column, held press conferences, and served as the U.S. delegate to the United Nations. At the U.N., she was head of the Commission on Human Rights. Known and loved the world over, Eleanor Roosevelt was called "The First Lady of the World."

JACQUELINE BOUVIER KENNEDY (b. 1929)
Jackie Kennedy, the wife of 35th president John F. Kennedy, brought cultural programs and an historic renovation to the White House. She educated Americans in the history of the White House when she conducted the first televised tour of the newly restored house.

CLAUDIA TAYLOR JOHNSON (b. 1912)
The wife of Lyndon Johnson, the 36th president, was known to the country as "Lady Bird." She toured the U.S. campaigning for a more beautiful America, and lecturing on ways to improve the environment. It was her suggestion to beautify the roadsides by removing billboards and planting trees and flowers.

ROSALYNN SMITH CARTER (b. 1927)
Rosalynn Carter, the wife of 39th president Jimmy Carter, was the first lady to represent the administration on visits to foreign countries on her own. She also worked hard for mental health programs and for passage of the Equal Rights Amendment.

NANCY DAVIS REAGAN (b. 1923)
This first lady, the wife of the 40th president, Ronald Reagan, traveled throughout the U.S. talking to young people about her anti-drug campaign, "Say No to Drugs."

Ten Facts about the White House

The White House is the official home and office for the president of the United States. The house and grounds cover eighteen acres in Washington, D.C. Today, the house consists of 132 rooms, which include a barbershop, movie theater, gymnasium, pool, bowling alley, and five elevators. However, when the White House was first built it looked very different. Below is a brief history of the White House.

1. Every president except George Washington has lived in the White House. He chose the site for it, but the house was not completed until the end of his term of office. When Washington was president, he lived in homes in New York and Philadelphia, the first U.S. capital cities.

2. President John Adams and his family were the first to live in the White House. When they moved into the house in November 1780, there were only six rooms and an unfinished stairway. Abigail Adams did the housecleaning and dried the family wash on a line in the East Room. She had difficulty getting enough wood to keep the fireplaces burning and the house warm.

3. The house was first known as the "Presidential Palace." President Thomas Jefferson renamed it the "Executive Mansion." It was first called the "White House" when President Andrew Jackson lived there. In 1902, President Theodore Roosevelt made the name "White House" official, using an engraving of it on his stationery.

4. The White House was burned to a shell by the British army during the War of 1812. President Madison and his family moved to another house in Washington, D.C., while the White House was rebuilt.

5. Running water was first piped into the White House in 1833 when Andrew Jackson was president.

6. President Millard Fillmore installed an iron cookstove to replace the fireplace for cooking in 1850.

7. Alexander Graham Bell personally installed one of the country's first telephones in the White House for President Rutherford Hayes in 1877.

8. The first elevator (hand cranked) was installed by President Chester Arthur in 1881.

9. President Benjamin Harrison had the White House wired for electricity in 1891. It was one of the first homes in the country with electricity.

10. President Franklin Delano Roosevelt further modernized the White House kitchen by installing electric stoves and dishwashers during his term of office.

Little-Known Facts about George Washington

• George Washington never shook hands with people, not even with his friends. As president, he officially greeted people with a bow.

• Washington had his own household silver candlesticks melted down into coins for the first U.S. mint.

• George Washington had no children of his own, but he was a father to his two stepchildren, John (Jack) and Martha (Patsy). When Jack died at the age of 26, George and Martha Washington adopted and raised the grandchildren, George (Little Wash) and Nellie.

• Although he was a wealthy man, Washington had to borrow money for the trip to New York for his first inauguration. At that time, his money had been invested in his land.

• It is true that George Washington had false teeth. However, they were not made of wood but hippopotamus ivory. He lost his real teeth because of a poor diet.

Little-Known Facts about Abraham Lincoln

• Abraham Lincoln was the first president to wear a beard. He grew it at the request of a twelve-year-old girl, Grace Bedell, who wrote and told him that he would look better with a beard because his face was so thin.

• Lincoln so loved home-baked pies that the ladies of New Salem, Illinois, frequently mailed their pies (usually apple) to him while he lived at the White House.

• President Lincoln was the first to proclaim Thanksgiving Day as a national holiday.

• Abraham Lincoln was the first U.S. president born outside of the original thirteen states. He was born in Hodgenville, Kentucky, and moved to Illinois, the state from which he was elected.

• Lincoln and his wife, Mary, had four children, Robert, Edward, William, and Thomas (Tad). Three of his sons died young; only Robert survived to adulthood.

Presidents Who Were Related

• John Adams, the second president, was the father of John Quincy Adams, the sixth president.

• James Madison, the fourth president, was second cousin to Zachary Taylor, the twelfth president.

• William Henry Harrison, the ninth president, was the grandfather of Benjamin Harrison, the 23rd president.

• Theodore Roosevelt, the 26th president, was the fifth cousin of Franklin Delano Roosevelt, the 32nd president.

Religion

This is a helpful guide to major world religions, including sacred books, places of worship, and religious people.

Religions of the World

BUDDHISM

• Founded about 500 B.C. by Prince Siddhartha Gautama (the Buddha) near Benares, India.

• Practiced mainly in Ceylon, Japan, and India.

• The symbol of this religion is an eight-spoked wheel. Each spoke represents a step toward peace of mind and an end to suffering. It is called the "eightfold path."

Step 1—Right knowledge
Step 2—Right intention
Step 3—Right speech
Step 4—Right conduct
Step 5—Right means of livelihood
Step 6—Right effort
Step 7—Right mindfulness
Step 8—Right concentration

• The sacred book is the *Tripitaka*, a collection of Buddha's teachings.

• There are no gods, but Buddhists worship images of Buddha.

• Followers practice yoga and meditation.

• Buddhists believe that people are born and reborn over and over again. When they achieve enlightenment they are finally freed from all desire and the cycle of rebirth. They have then reached Nirvana.

CHRISTIANITY

• Founded by the followers of Jesus Christ after A.D. 4.

• The most popular religion in the world. Over one-fifth of world's population follows one of its sects.

• Practiced mainly in Europe, North America, and South America.

• The holy book is the *Bible* which consists of the Old Testament and New Testament (Christ's life and teachings).

• There are hundreds of Christian groups called denominations. Their beliefs and practices vary.

• Christians believe in one God and in Jesus Christ as the son of God. God redeemed the sins of humans when Jesus Christ was crucified and died on the cross. Jesus then ascended into heaven as the son of God.

• In Christian teaching, the soul lives after the body dies. The soul goes to heaven to live with God or to hell for eternal damnation.

CONFUCIANISM

- Founded in China in the 6th century B.C. by Confucius (K'ung Fu-tzu).
- Practiced in China, Japan, and Mongolia.
- Believe in heaven, ancestor worship, and many gods.
- Sacred books are the *Analects* (*Lun Yu*) and the *Wu Ching* (fire classics), ancient Chinese writings.
- Believe in afterlife with ancestors in heaven.
- No clergy.

HINDUISM

- Began c. 1500 B.C.; the founder is unknown.
- Practiced mainly in India.
- Hindus are born to their religion. There are no converts.
- The sacred text is the *Veda*, a collection of myths, epic stories, and rituals.
- There are hundreds of gods and goddesses, enough so that each family has a favorite to honor.
- Followers believe in a cycle of birth and rebirth. Each life is determined by past deeds called Karma. (The concept of Karma is also shared by Buddhists.)

ISLAM

- Founded in A.D. 610 by Muhammed in Mecca, Arabia.
- Followers of Islam are called Muslims (which in Arabic means one who submits to the will of Allah).

- The holy book is the *Koran*.
- Islam means submission to the will of Allah. According to the teachings of Islam, the universe belongs to Allah.
- The five pillars of faith of Islam are:
    1. Believing in Allah.
    2. Praying 5 times a day.
    3. Donating to charity.
    4. Fasting during the month of Ramadan.
    5. Making a pilgrimage to Mecca at least once in a lifetime.

JUDAISM

- Founded by Abraham nearly 5,000 years ago.
- The major areas of practice are Israel, the U.S., and the U.S.S.R.
- The holy book is the *Torah* (the first five books of the Old Testament).
- Followers believe in one God, Jehovah, who is the creator and ruler of the Universe.
- Jews believe their souls will live forever.

TAOISM

- Founded in 600 B.C. by Lao-Tze in China.
- Practiced mainly in China.
- The sacred book is the *Tao-te-Ching*.
- Tao means a way or a road.
- Followers believe in the yin and yang of the Universe. *Yin* represents the earth; *yang* represents heaven. The balance of yin and yang gives order to the world. People are encouraged to work in harmony with nature.

Original Language of Sacred Books

Book	Language	Religion
Koran	Arabic	Islam
New Testament	Greek	Christianity
Old Testament	Hebrew	Judaism
Tripitaka	Pali (Old Indian Language)	Buddhism
Veda	Sanskrit	Hinduism

Origins of Religious Traditions

Kneeling—Symbolizes man's submission to a higher power. While kneeling, the body as well as the mind worships. Common in Christianity and Islam.

Covering of the Head—Originated as a method for driving off evil spirits. Today, worshippers cover their heads as a symbol of respect.

Amen—A widely-used religious word. It is Hebrew for "so be it."

Religious People and Places of Worship

Religion	People	Place
Buddhism	Monks, Nuns	Temple
Christianity	Priests, Ministers	Church
Hinduism	Gurus (teachers), Sadhus	Temple
Islam	Imam (prayer leader), Muezzin (prayer chanter)	Mosque
Judaism	Rabbi, Cantor	Synagogue

Sports

Here's a winning lineup of sports shorts including: memorable events, young athletes, stats, records, popular sports around the world, sports in books and movies, and how you can write to your favorite athlete.

Long-Standing Sports Records

These sports records have stood for many years and will probably last for years to come. But remember, records are made to be broken.

OLYMPICS

100-meter run—Jim Hines, 9.9 seconds, 1968

400-meter run—Lee Evans, 43.8 seconds, 1968

Long jump—Bob Beamon, 29 ft. 2½ in., 1968 (also world record)

COLLEGE BASKETBALL
(DIVISION 1)

Highest career scoring average—Pete Maravich, Louisiana State University, 44.2 points per game, 1968, 1969, 1970

Highest points per game average in a season—Pete Maravich, Louisiana State University, 44.5 points per game, 1969-70

Most consecutive championships—University of California, Los Angeles, 7, 1967-73

NATIONAL BASKETBALL ASSOCIATION

Most consecutive championships—Boston Celtics, 8, 1959-66

Highest points per game average in a season—Wilt Chamberlain, 50.4, 1962

Most consecutive scoring titles—Wilt Chamberlain, 7, 1960-66

Most rebounds in a game—Wilt Chamberlain, 55, 1963

Most points in a game—Wilt Chamberlain, 100, 1962

COLLEGE FOOTBALL
(DIVISION I)

Longest winning streak—University of Oklahoma, 47 games, 1953-57

Most points scored in a game—Jim Brown, Syracuse University, 43, 1956

NATIONAL FOOTBALL LEAGUE

Most touchdowns scored—Jim Brown, 106, 1957-65

Most touchdowns rushing in a game—Ernie Nevers, 6, 1929

Most yards passing in a game—Norm Van Brocklin, 554, 1951

Most touchdown receptions—Don Hutson, 99, 1935-45

Most points scored in a season—Paul Hornung, 176, 1960

Most interceptions in a season—Dick "Night Train" Lane, 14, 1952

MAJOR LEAGUE BASEBALL

Longest consecutive-game hitting streak—Joe DiMaggio, 56 games, 1941

Highest batting average in a season—Rogers Hornsby, .424, 1924

Last major leaguer to bat .400 or better in a season—Ted Williams, 1941

Most home runs in a season—Roger Maris, 61, 1961

Most National League home runs in a season—Hack Wilson, 56, 1930

Most hits in a world series—Bobby Richardson, 13, 1964 (tied by Marty Barrett, 1986)

Most walks allowed in a world series game—Babe Ruth, 11, 1926

Most consecutive major league games won—Carl Hubbell, 24, 1936-37

Most shutouts in a season—Grover Cleveland Alexander, 16, 1916

Most hits in a season—George Sisler, 257, 1920

Most runs batted in for one season—Hack Wilson, 190, 1930

Most doubles in a season—Earl Webb, 67, 1931

Most triples in a season—Owen Wilson, 36, 1912

Most consecutive games played—Lou Gehrig, 2,130, 1925-39

Memorable Events in Sports

These once-in-a-lifetime achievements brought fame to the individuals and teams who will always be remembered for these special moments.

100 POINTS

Wilt Chamberlain of the Philadelphia Warriors scored one hundred points in a game against the New York Knickerbockers at Hershey, Pennsylvania, on March 2, 1962. He set the National Basketball Association record by scoring 36 field goals and making 28 free throws.

LUCKY SEVEN
Bill Walton, sinking twenty-one of twenty-two field goal attempts, scored a record forty-one points against Memphis State University in the 1973 NCAA championship basketball game to lead the University of California, Los Angeles, to a 87-66 victory. It was the seventh consecutive basketball championship for UCLA.

OLYMPIC HEROES
Mark Spitz, American swimmer, won a record seven gold medals at the 1972 Olympic Games. He set four world records in individual swimming events. Jesse Owens was the first track & field athlete to win four Olympic gold medals. He accomplished the feat at the 1936 Olympic Games in Berlin, Germany.

PERFECT!
Don Larsen of the New York Yankees pitched a perfect game against the Brooklyn Dodgers in the 1956 World Series. He is the only pitcher to hurl a World Series perfect game.

ALMOST PERFECT
Harvey Haddix of the Pittsburgh Pirates pitched a perfect game for twelve innings against the Milwaukee Braves on May 26, 1959. He allowed a hit in the thirteenth inning and lost the game.

AMAZIN'!
The New York Mets, losing by two runs with two out and nobody on base in the bottom of the tenth inning, rallied to score three runs to win the sixth game of the 1986 World Series. In another come-from-behind effort, the Mets defeated the Boston Red Sox in the seventh game to win the championship.

THE SHOT HEARD AROUND THE WORLD.
With the Brooklyn Dodgers leading 4-2 with one out in the ninth inning of the third and final game of the 1951 National League playoffs, Bobby Thomson hit a three-run homer to give the New York Giants the 1951 National League pennant. Thomson's homer capped a pennant drive that began with the Giants 13½ games behind the Dodgers on August 12.

"I GUARANTEE IT."
The New York Jets, led by quarterback Joe Namath, upset the heavily favored Baltimore Colts to win the 1969 Super Bowl. It was the first victory for an American Football League team in the championship game and completely altered the face of professional football.

PITTSBURGH STEALER
Terry Bradshaw of the Pittsburgh Steelers threw a pass that was deflected by the Oakland Raiders defensive back Jack Tatum into the hands of Steeler Franco Harris who ran forty-two yards for a touchdown with five seconds remaining in the game. The pass, which has been called the "immaculate reception," gave the Steelers a 13-7 victory over the Raiders in the first round of the American Football Conference playoffs.

Notable Feats by Young Athletes

Baseball

• **Joe Nuxhall** played major league baseball with the Cincinnati Reds in 1944 at age fifteen.

Basketball

• **Bill Willoughby** became the youngest National Basketball Association player when he made his debut with the Atlanta Hawks when he was eighteen years, five months, and three days old.

Boxing

• **Wilfredo Benitez** became the youngest boxing champion when he won the WBA Light Welterweight Championship in 1976 at the age of seventeen.

• **Mike Tyson**, at age twenty years, four months, and twenty-two days, became the youngest heavyweight boxing champion in 1986.

Horse Racing

• **Steve Cauthen**, at age eighteen, won thoroughbred racing's Triple Crown in 1978 by riding Affirmed to victories in the Kentucky Derby, Preakness, and Belmont Stakes.

• **Frank Wooten**, British jockey, rode his first winner at age nine.

Olympics

• **Bob Mathias**, the youngest male Olympic gold medalist, won the 1948 decathlon at age seventeen years, 263 days.

• **Barbara Jones** was a member of the 1952 United States Olympic 4 x 100 relay team when she won a gold medal at age fifteen years, 123 days.

Rodeo

• **Metha Brorsen** won the 1975 International Rodeo cowgirls barrel racing title at age eleven.

Tennis

• **Tracy Austin** became the youngest champion in the history of the U.S. Open Tennis Championship when she won the 1979 women's singles title at age sixteen.

• **Boris Becker** of West Germany became the youngest men's singles tennis champion at Wimbledon (All-England Championship) at age seventeen.

Popular Sports Around the World

Soccer is the most popular sport in the world. It is called football in most parts of the world, but is called soccer in the United States and Canada. Below is a list of sports and those nations in which they are especially popular.

Badminton: India, Malaysia, Thailand

Baseball: United States, Caribbean islands, Japan

Basketball: United States, Mexico, U.S.S.R., Italy

Bicycle Racing: France, Italy, West Germany

Bobsledding: East Germany, West Germany, Switzerland
Boccie (lawn bowling): Italy
Cricket: Great Britain, Australia
Curling: Canada
Fencing: France, Italy, West Germany
Golf: United States, Great Britain

Gymnastics: U.S.S.R., Japan, China, United States, Romania
Harness Racing: United States, Australia
Hockey, Field: India, Pakistan, West Germany
Hockey, Ice: United States, Canada, U.S.S.R., Sweden, Finland

Hurling: Ireland
Judo: Japan, South Korea
Lacrosse: United States, Canada
Luge: Italy, East Germany
Polo: Argentina, India, Australia, Great Britain
Rowing: Canada, Romania, Great Britain, United States
Rugby: Great Britain
Skiing, Alpine: Switzerland, Italy, Sweden
Skiing, Nordic: Norway, Finland, Sweden
Speed Ice Skating: U.S.S.R., Canada, East Germany, Sweden
Swimming: United States, East Germany, Australia
Table Tennis: China, Japan
Tennis: United States, Great Britain, Australia, Czechoslovakia, Sweden
Volleyball: United States, China, U.S.S.R.

Sports Numbers

In these "games of inches," it is valuable to know these measurements.

Major League Baseball

Circumference of ball—Not less than 9 in. nor more than 9¼ in.
Weight of ball—Not less than 5 nor more than 5¼ oz.

Bat—Must be round, not over 2¾ in. in diameter at thickest part; not more than 42 in. in length.

Home plate to pitching rubber—60 ft., 6 in.

Home plate to second base—127 ft. 3⅜ in.

Base to base—90 ft.

Home plate—17 in. x 12 in. x 12 in., cut to a point at the rear.

Batter's box—4 ft. x 6 ft.

Pitching rubber—24 in. x 6 in.

Bases—15 in. x 15 in.

Professional Football

Field—360 ft. (100 yds.) long x 160 ft. wide; end zones are 30 ft. (10 yds.) deep.

Ball—Weight, 14-15 oz.; length, 11-11¼ in.

Goal posts—18 ft., 6 in. wide; top face of crossbar must be 10 ft. above the ground; vertical posts must extend at least 30 ft. above the crossbar.

Professional Basketball

Weight of ball—Not less than 20 nor more than 22 oz.

Circumference of ball—30 in.

Playing court—94 ft. x 50 ft.

Baskets—Rims 18 in. in inside diameter; rim itself not more than ⅝ in. in diameter.

Height of basket—10 ft.

Free throw line—15 ft. from the backboard, 3 in. wide.

National Hockey League

Size of puck—1 in. thick and 3 in. in diameter; weight 5½ to 6 oz.

Size of goal—6 ft. wide x 4 ft. in height.

Size of rink—200 ft. long x 85 ft. wide (this may vary).

Length of stick—Skater's stick not more than 58 in. from heel to end of shaft nor 12½ in. from heel to end of blade; blade cannot be more than 3 in. in width but not less than 2 in. Goalie's stick cannot exceed 3½ in. in width except at the heel, where it must not exceed 4½ in.

Other Sports Numbers

Bowling alley—foul line to head pin, 60 ft.

Polo field—300 yds. long x 200 yds. wide.

Ping pong table—9 ft. long x 5 ft. wide.

Tennis court—78 ft. long x 27 ft. wide (singles) or 36 ft. wide (doubles).

Tennis net—3 ft. high in center; 3½ ft. high at net posts.

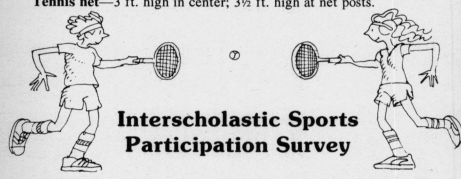

Interscholastic Sports Participation Survey

Below are the sports in which senior high school students participate, based on a survey by the National Federation of State High School Associations for the 1984-85 school year.

Boys		Girls	
Sport	*Participants*	*Sport*	*Participants*
Football	1,006,675	Basketball	389,230
Basketball	493,806	Track & Field (outdoor)	344,730
Track & Field (outdoor)	455,277	Volleyball	259,827
Baseball	391,810	Softball(fast pitch)	208,177
Wrestling	244,598	Tennis	117,170
Soccer	180,281	Cross Country	94,879

Boys		Girls	
Sport	**Participants**	**Sport**	**Participants**
Cross Country	155,550	Swimming & Diving	77,268
Tennis	124,467	Soccer	75,944
Golf	107,155	Field Hockey	50,313
Swimming & Diving	78,256	Gymnastics	35,440

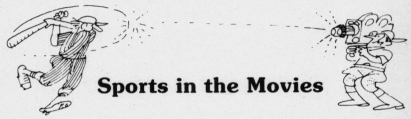

Sports in the Movies

There have been many noteworthy sports movies, most of them about baseball and boxing. Some noteworthy movies about sports and sports heroes are listed below.

Baseball Films

Baseball has been the theme for movies such as: *Angels in the Out-field, The Natural, Damn Yankees, It Happens Every Spring, Take Me Out to the Ballgame,* and *The Bad News Bears.*

BASEBALL BIOGRAPHIES:

- **The Stratton Story** (Monty Stratton)
- **The Babe Ruth Story**
- **The Pride of the Yankees** (Lou Gehrig)
- **The Pride of St. Louis** (Dizzy Dean)
- **The Winning Team** (starring Ronald Reagan as Grover Cleveland Alexander)
- **The Jackie Robinson Story** (starring Jackie Robinson as himself)

Boxing Films

Notable fictionalized boxing films include: *The Champ, Body and Soul, Golden Boy, The Harder They Fall, The Great White Hope,* and the *Rocky* movies.

BOXERS' BIOGRAPHIES:

- **Gentleman Jim** (Jim Corbett)
- **The Great John L.** (John L. Sullivan)
- **The Joe Louis Story**
- **Somebody Up There Likes Me** (Rocky Graziano)
- **Raging Bull** (Jake La Motta)

Football Films

- Probably the most famous football movie is *Knute Rockne, All American*, with Pat O'Brien as Rockne and Ronald Reagan as George Gipp. The film contains the phrase "Win one for the Gipper."
- Another noteworthy football movie is *Brian's Song*, which starred James Caan as the Chicago Bears running back, Brian Piccolo.
- Still another was *Jim Thorpe—All American*, which starred Burt Lancaster as the legendary Indian athlete.

10 Good Books about Sports

Fiction

1. **The Contender**—by Robert Lipsyte (boxing)
2. **Hoops**—by Walter Dean Myers (basketball)
3. **In the Year of the Boar and Jackie Robinson**—by Bette Bao Lord (baseball)
4. **Zanballer**—by R.R. Knudson (football)

Non-fiction

5. **Baseball's Best: The MVPs**—by Dave Masterson and Timm Boyle
6. **Football for Young Players and Parents**—by Joe Namath
7. **Hoosiers: The Fabulous Basketball Life of Indiana**—by Phillip M. Hoose
8. **Everybody's Hockey Book**—by Stan and Shirley Fischler
9. **Soccer for Juniors: A Guide for Players, Parents, and Coaches**—by Robert Pollock
10. **Winning Women: The Changing Image of Women in Sports**—by Tony Duffy and Paul Wade

Write to Your Favorite Athlete

Most professional athletes enjoy hearing from their fans. If you would like to write to your favorite sports hero, you may send the letter to the player in care of his team. Listed below are the addresses of the major league baseball teams and the teams of the National Football League, the National Basketball Association, and the National Hockey League.

BASEBALL

National League

National League Office
350 Park Ave.
New York, NY 10022

Atlanta Braves
P.O. Box 4064
Atlanta, GA 30302

Chicago Cubs
Wrigley Field
Chicago, IL 60613

Cincinnati Reds
100 Riverfront Stadium
Cincinnati, OH 45202

Houston Astros
Astrodome
Houston, TX 77001

Los Angeles Dodgers
Dodger Stadium
Los Angeles, CA 90012

Montreal Expos
P.O. Box 500, Station M
Montreal, Quebec H1V 3P2
Canada

New York Mets
Shea Stadium
Flushing, NY 11368

Philadelphia Phillies
P.O. Box 7575
Philadelphia, PA 19101

Pittsburgh Pirates
Three Rivers Stadium
Pittsburgh, PA 15212

St. Louis Cardinals
Busch Stadium
St. Louis, MO 63102

San Diego Padres
P.O. Box 2000
San Diego, CA 92120

San Francisco Giants
Candlestick Park
San Francisco, CA 94124

American League

American League Office
350 Park Ave.
New York, NY 10022

Baltimore Orioles
Memorial Stadium
Baltimore, MD 21218

Boston Red Sox
24 Yawkey Way
Boston, MA 02215

California Angels
Anaheim Stadium
Anaheim, CA 92806

Chicago White Sox
324 W. 35th St.
Chicago, IL 60616

Cleveland Indians
Cleveland Stadium
Cleveland, OH 44114

Detroit Tigers
Tiger Stadium
Detroit, MI 48216

Kansas City Royals
Harry S. Truman Sports Complex
Kansas City, MO 64141

Milwaukee Brewers
Milwaukee County Stadium
Milwaukee, WI 53214

Minnesota Twins
501 Chicago Ave. South
Minneapolis, MN 55415

New York Yankees
Yankee Stadium
Bronx, NY 10451

Oakland A's
Oakland Coliseum
Oakland, CA 94621

Seattle Mariners
100 S. King St.
Seattle, WA 98104

Texas Rangers
1200 Copeland Rd.
Arlington, TX 76011

Toronto Blue Jays
Box 7777
Adelaide St. P.O.
Toronto, Ontario
M5C 2K7 Canada

NATIONAL FOOTBALL LEAGUE

League Office
410 Park Avenue
New York, NY 10022

Atlanta Falcons
Suwanee Road
Suwanee, GA 30174

Buffalo Bills
1 Bills Drive
Orchard Park, NY 14127

Chicago Bears
250 N. Washington
Lake Forest, IL 60045

Cincinnati Bengals
200 Riverfront Stadium
Cincinnati, OH 45202

Cleveland Browns
Cleveland Stadium
Cleveland, OH 44114

Dallas Cowboys
One Cowboy Pkwy.
Irving, TX 75063

Denver Broncos
5700 Logan St.
Denver, CO 80216

Detroit Lions
1200 Featherstone Rd.
Pontiac, MI 48057

Green Bay Packers
1265 Lombardi Ave.
Green Bay, WI 54307

Houston Oilers
P.O. Box 1516
Houston, TX 77001

Indianapolis Colts
P.O. Box 54000
Indianapolis, IN 46254

Kansas City Chiefs
1 Arrowhead Drive
Kansas City, MO 64129

Los Angeles Raiders
332 Center St.
El Segundo, CA 90245

Los Angeles Rams
2327 W. Lincoln Ave.
Anaheim, CA 92801

Miami Dolphins
4770 Biscayne Blvd.
Miami, FL 33137

Minnesota Vikings
9520 Viking Dr.
Eden Prairie, MN 55344

New England Patriots
Sullivan Stadium
Foxboro, MA 02035

New Orleans Saints
1500 Poydras St.
New Orleans, LA 70112

New York Giants
Giants Stadium
E. Rutherford, NJ 07073

New York Jets
598 Madison Ave.
New York, NY 10022

Philadelphia Eagles
Veterans Stadium
Philadelphia, PA 19148

Pittsburgh Steelers
Three Rivers Stadium
Pittsburgh, PA 15212

St. Louis Cardinals
Busch Stadium
St. Louis, MO 63188

San Diego Chargers
P.O. Box 20666
San Diego, CA 92120

San Francisco 49ers
711 Nevada St.
Redwood City, CA 94061

Seattle Seahawks
5305 Lake Washington Blvd.
Kirkland, WA 98033

Tampa Bay Buccaneers
1 Buccaneer Place
Tampa, FL 33607

Washington Redskins
P.O. Box 17247
Dulles Intl. Airport
Washington, DC 20041

NATIONAL BASKETBALL ASSOCIATION

League Office
645 5th Ave.
New York, NY 10022

Atlanta Hawks
100 Techwood Drive NW
Atlanta, GA 30303

Boston Celtics
Boston Garden
Boston, MA 02114

Chicago Bulls
980 North Michigan Ave.
Chicago, IL 60611

Cleveland Cavaliers
2923 Statesboro Rd.
Richfield, OH 44286

Dallas Mavericks
777 Sports St.
Dallas, TX 75207

Denver Nuggets
1635 Clay St.
Denver, CO 80204

Detroit Pistons
1200 Featherstone
Pontiac, MI 48057

Golden State Warriors
Oakland Coliseum
Oakland, CA 94621

Houston Rockets
The Summit
Houston, TX 77046

Indiana Pacers
2 W. Washington St.
Indianapolis, IN 46204

Los Angeles Clippers
3939 Figueroa
Los Angeles, CA 90037

Los Angeles Lakers
P.O. Box 10
Inglewood, CA 90306

Milwaukee Bucks
901 North 4th St.
Milwaukee, WI 53203

New Jersey Nets
Meadowlands Arena
E. Rutherford, NJ 07073

New York Knickerbockers
4 Pennsylvania Plaza
New York, NY 10001

Philadelphia 76ers
P.O. Box 25040
Philadelphia, PA 19147

Phoenix Suns
2910 N. Central
Phoenix, AZ 85012

Portland Trail Blazers
700 NE Multnomah St.
Portland, OR 97232

Sacramento Kings
1515 Sports Dr.
Sacramento, CA 95834

San Antonio Spurs
P.O. Box 530
San Antonio, TX 78292

Seattle SuperSonics
190 Queen Ann Ave. N
Seattle, WA 98109

Utah Jazz
5 Triad Center
Salt Lake City, UT 84180

Washington Bullets
Capital Centre
Landover, MD 20785

NATIONAL HOCKEY LEAGUE

League Headquarters
Sun Life Bldg.
Montreal, Quebec H3B 2W2
Canada

Boston Bruins
150 Causeway St.
Boston, MA 02114

Buffalo Sabres
Memorial Auditorium
Buffalo, NY 14202

Calgary Flames
P.O. Box 1540
Calgary, Alta. T2P 3B9
Canada

Chicago Black Hawks
1800 W. Madison St.
Chicago, IL 60612

Detroit Red Wings
600 Civic Center Drive
Detroit, MI 48226

Edmonton Oilers
Northlands Coliseum
Edmonton, Alta. T5B 4M9
Canada

Hartford Whalers
One Civic Center Plaza
Hartford, CT 06103

Los Angeles Kings
P.O. Box 10
Inglewood, CA 90306

Minnesota North Stars
7901 Cedar Ave. S.
Bloomington, MN 55420

Montreal Canadiens
2313 St. Catherine St., West
Montreal, Quebec H3H 1N2
Canada

New Jersey Devils
Meadowlands Arena
E. Rutherford, NJ 07073

New York Islanders
Nassau Coliseum
Uniondale, NY 11553

New York Rangers
4 Pennsylvania Plaza
New York, NY 10001

Philadelphia Flyers
Pattison Place
Philadelphia, PA 19148

Pittsburgh Penguins
Civic Arena
Pittsburgh, PA 15219

Quebec Nordiques
2205 Ave. du Colisee
Quebec, Quebec G1L 4W7
Canada

St. Louis Blues
5700 Oakland Ave.
St. Louis, MO 63110

Toronto Maple Leafs
60 Carlton St.
Toronto, Ont. M5B 1L1
Canada

Vancouver Canucks
100 North Renfrew St.
Vancouver, B.C. V5K 3N7
Canada

Washington Capitals
Capital Centre
Landover, MD 20785

Winnipeg Jets
15-1430 Maroons Road
Winnipeg, Man. R3G 0L5
Canada

Testing

Do you hate tests? Lots of people do. But tests are a fact of life. If you know why you're taking a test, what kind of test it is, and the best way to take it, your results will probably be better. And if you still don't come out at the top of your class, it might help to know that some of the greatest geniuses in the history of the world have flunked tests or done poorly in school!

Five Terrific Reasons for Taking Tests

1. Tests can help teachers know you better, so they can decide what courses you are doing well in, and at what level.

2. Tests can help teachers decide whether you need special help.

3. Tests can help teachers find out how well they are teaching. For example, if half your class answers a question or a series of questions incorrectly, the teacher will know to teach that lesson again.

4. Tests can help you find out what you know and what you need to study more. Ask your teacher, or have your parents ask your teacher for this information.

5. Tests can help you compare your progress with your classmates, so you know you either need to work harder or you can pat yourself on the back and relax a little.

Four Kinds of Standardized Tests

1. **Intelligence tests** measure general problem-solving ability. They are made up of many different kinds of questions. For example, you might be asked to look at an incomplete picture and tell what is missing, or to arrange a series of pictures so that they tell a story.

2. **Aptitude tests** break down intelligence into special areas, such as mathematical, verbal, scientific, and artistic. They measure how much you might be capable of learning in each area.

3. **Achievement tests** are cousins of aptitude tests. They measure how much you have already learned in specific areas. A verbal achievement test, for example, might evaluate your vocabulary and your ability to read, spell, and write grammatically.

4. **Psychological tests** compare your personality with others. There are many different types of personality tests. On one type of test, for example, you may be asked to answer True or False to the statement: "I consider myself a leader."

15 Tips on Taking Tests

BEFORE THE TEST

1. Never wait until the last minute to study for a test. Use the night before the test for review.

2. Keep old tests. Most teachers like certain kinds of questions, and you'll do better if you know what to expect.

3. To find out if you really know the material, try to teach it to somebody else. If you have a friend who's good at part of a subject and you're good at another part, get together and teach each other.

4. Practice for the test. Ask somebody to give you a sample test, so you can find out whether you know the answers. You'll also get used to taking the test.

5. Get a good night's sleep the night before the test.

6. Dress comfortably.

7. Have a good breakfast the morning of a test, and if the test is in the afternoon, don't eat too much sugar or junk food at lunchtime.

8. Bring everything you'll need to take the test, such as sharp pencils with erasers, so you won't waste time borrowing.

DURING THE TEST

9. Make sure you understand the instructions. If you don't, ask the teacher or test monitor for help.

10. Don't rush.

11. When answering a multiple-choice question, read all the possible answers before making your choice.

12. If you don't know the answer to a multiple-choice question, you should guess the answer *only if* you can narrow down the possibilities to two.

13. If you can't answer a question at all, skip it and go on to the next one.

14. If you erase an answer, do it thoroughly and neatly.

15. After you've answered the last question, if there's still time, go back and try to answer any questions you missed.

Seven Achievers Who Flunked Tests

1. ALBERT EINSTEIN

As a child, Einstein was dyslexic (he read letters backwards), and he showed little scholastic ability. He left school at 15 with no diploma and poor grades in history, geography, and languages. At 16, when he first applied to the Polytechnic Institute in Zurich, Switzerland, he failed the entrance exam. Einstein grew up to become one of the greatest theoretical physicists of all time, with one of the most creative intellects in human history.

2. ISAAC NEWTON

A lackluster student, Newton graduated from Trinity College at Cambridge University without honors or distinction. Yet, Newton had one of the greatest scientific minds in history. All modern science and technology stem from his work.

3. THOMAS EDISON

The most famous inventor of all time went to school for only three months. After his teacher called the eight-year-old Edison "addled," meaning that his mind was confused, his mother pulled him out of school and taught him at home. By the time he was nine, his experiments had gone far beyond his mother's understanding. Among his more than 1,000 inventions were the electric light and phonograph, and he helped perfect motion pictures, the telephone, and the electric generator.

4. BENJAMIN FRANKLIN

This famous American failed arithmetic as a boy. His father took Franklin out of school at age 10 and put him to work cutting wicks and melting tallow in the family's candle and soap shop. Franklin grew up to serve his nation as a great statesman, scientist, and public leader. Thomas Jefferson called Franklin, "The greatest man and ornament of the age and country in which he lived."

5. CHARLES DARWIN

Young Darwin did so badly at school that his father took him out, saying, "You care for nothing but shooting, dogs, and rat catching, and you will be a disgrace to yourself and all your family." Afterward, Darwin was sent to study medicine, which nauseated him. He was then sent to study for the ministry, but he spent his time with young sportsmen instead. Yet, Darwin grew up to revolutionize the science of biology.

6. SENATOR EDWARD M. KENNEDY
This Massachusetts senator and one-time presidential candidate was suspended from Harvard University because a friend took an exam for him.

7. SIR WINSTON CHURCHILL
Author, artist, statesman, and prime minister of England, Churchill failed the entrance exam for the Royal Military College not once, but *twice*.

Transportation and Travel

Let your imagination take you around the world on incredible journeys with remarkable people in all kinds of vehicles. Learn amazing facts about tremendous trucks and well-known cars. It's all here, so get going!

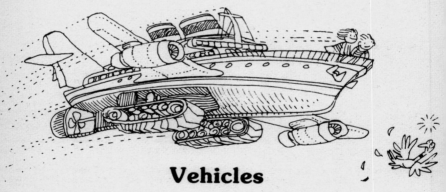

Vehicles

Ambulance   A vehicle used to carry people to the hospital. The first ambulance was invented in 1792 by Baron Dominique Jean Larrey, Napoleon's personal surgeon. The ambulance was a two-wheeled horse-drawn carriage with springs. It was used to carry the wounded off the battlefield comfortably.

Blimp   A nonrigid airship, also called a dirigible. It is wingless, has an engine, and can be steered with a rudder.

Chariot The first known wheeled vehicle. Used by many ancient peoples, it was a two-wheeled car open at the back. Donkeys were first used to pull chariots, then horses.

Double-decker bus A bus with an upper and lower passenger area. These buses were first built in London in 1847 to make room for the many people who wanted to travel by bus. Double-decker buses are still used today throughout England.

18-Wheeler A large tractor and trailer with 18 tires.

Ferryboat A boat used to carry passengers, vehicles, or goods across a body of water. Most run by engines; others are pulled by animals or people located on a nearby shore or riverbank.

Glider An airplane without an engine. The glider is usually towed up into the air by an engine-powered plane. When released, it floats on air currents.

Hovercraft A wheelless vehicle that moves close to but above ground or water on a cushion of air. Also called an air-cushion vehicle (ACV).

Iceboat A narrow sailboat with runners that travels on ice instead of water.

Jeep A general purpose four-wheel drive vehicle. It was first designed for and used by the U.S. Army. "Jeep" is the shortened version of general purpose.

Kayak A type of canoe first made by Eskimos, consisting of a frame covered with animal skins with a small opening for the paddler.

Limousine A large luxurious sedan, often called a "limo." Many have a glass partition to separate the driver or chauffeur from the passengers.

Moped A cross between a bike and a motorcycle, a moped has both a motor and pedals.

Nuclear-powered submarines This type of submarine uses an atomic reactor to generate heat that drives a high-speed engine. The first nuclear-powered submarine, the *Nautilus,* was also the first sea vessel to sail beneath the North Pole.

Ocean liner A large ship that is like a floating hotel. There are restaurants, shops, theaters, exercise rooms, swimming pools, and elevators on modern ocean liners.

Paddle wheel boats A riverboat with a large wheel made of flat paddles which move the boat as they turn. A steam engine moves the paddles.

Q-Ship An armed ship disguised as a fishing or merchant ship and used as a decoy for enemy submarines.

Raft A collection of logs or timber tied together. Rafts were the first boats made by people.

Snowmobile A motor-driven vehicle on skis, used to move over snow and ice. In 1928, Ford Motor Company built snowmobiles for Admiral Byrd's polar expedition.

Tugboats Small, powerful boats used to tow and guide large boats and barges in narrow and shallow waters.

Unicycle A single-wheeled vehicle propelled by pedals.

Van A small, box-shaped truck with rear or side doors.

Wagon train A long line of covered wagons used by the American pioneers in their travels west. Many covered wagons were pulled by oxen.

Xebec   A three-masted sailing ship with a long, overhanging bow and stern. Pronounced "zee-beck."

Yawl   A ship's small boat, sometimes called the jolly boat. Also a type of sailboat.

Zeppelin   A rigid airship named after its inventor, Count Ferdinand von Zeppelin of Germany. The largest airship ever built was the *Hindenberg.*

Cars were once called horseless carriages as an insult. Names such as motor wagon, autobat, and trundler were suggested as labels for these vehicles. Finally, the French Academy convened to come up with the official name: automobile. The word "car" comes from the Latin *carries* which was a type of Roman chariot. Below are the origins of some modern car names.

Cadillac—Named after the founder of the city of Detroit, Antoine de la Mothe Cadillac.

Chevrolet—Named after Louis Chevrolet, an American automaker.

Chrysler—Named after Walter Chrysler, an American automaker.

Ford—Named after American automaker, Henry Ford.

Honda—Named after Doichiro Honda of Japan, a one-time auto repair shop owner who went on to develop and manufacture motorcycles, later founding the Honda Motor Company.

Lincoln—A Ford Motor Company car named in honor of President Abraham Lincoln.

Plymouth—Named in honor of the Pilgrims who arrived in Plymouth, Massachusetts, in 1620.

Pontiac—Named after Pontiac, an Ottowa Indian chief once renowned for his intelligence and cunning.

Tremendous Trucks

- The **crawler transporter** is the largest known overload vehicle. It is used by NASA to carry a space shuttle to its launching platform. The crawler is larger than a basketball court and moves on four double-tracked crawlers, each ten feet high and forty-one feet long.
- **Tires** for long, heavy trucks, such as mine dump trucks, must be large. Some are ten feet tall and cost over ten thousand dollars apiece. These tires are usually replaced every six months.
- **Tree crushers** are trucks used to clear dense forests. These trucks move at a top speed of three miles per hour on three wide barrel-shaped wheels.
- A **concrete truck** carries mixed concrete to where it is needed. The drum of the truck revolves during the trip to keep the concrete properly mixed. A concrete truck can carry up to twenty-eight tons of concrete, enough to build a wall three feet high, ninety feet long, and one foot thick.
- Different kinds of fire trucks serve different purposes for the firemen who use them:

  Pumpers are hose trucks with pumps.

  Ladder trucks only carry ladders and equipment to rescue people.

  Aerials are trucks with very long ladders that can be raised over one hundred feet to fight fires in tall buildings.

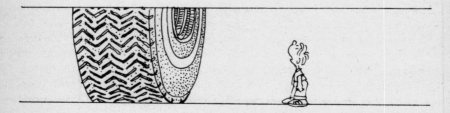

Remarkable Journeys

AROUND THE WORLD

In 1519, Ferdinand Magellan, a Portuguese navigator, set sail with five aged ships to circumnavigate the world. He sailed west from Spain under the patronage of the King of Spain. Two years later, he reached the Philippine islands in the West Pacific ocean, where he was killed by natives. A year later, in 1522, his surviving ship returned to Spain. This extraordinary voyage proved the theory that the earth was round.

AROUND THE WORLD—SOLO
In 1895, Captain Joshua Slocum of America set off alone in a twelve-ton sloop to sail around the world. Surviving gale winds, mighty waves, hostile pirate ships, and his on-board goat who ate his sailing charts, he returned to Newport, Rhode Island, in 1898. Slocum was the first to sail solo around the world. He did so with only a compass, a sextant, and a "dollar clock" as navigational tools.

ACROSS THE ATLANTIC
On May 20, 1927, Charles A. Lindbergh, Jr., took off in his plane, the *Spirit of St. Louis*, to fly from New York to Paris. He was not the first to fly across the Atlantic Ocean, but he was the first to do it alone. His flight began after Lindbergh had already been awake for twenty-four hours. On takeoff, his plane, weighted down with fuel, barely cleared a cluster of trees. Most of his flight was made by guesswork since his navigational instruments were so primitive, but when he finally sighted the European coast, he was only two miles off course. When he reached Paris 33½ hours after takeoff, he circled the Eiffel Tower three times to get his bearings. After he finished his 3,610-mile journey, he became world famous as the first to make a solo flight across the Atlantic Ocean.

ACROSS THE U.S.
In 1930, Americans Charles Creighton and James Hurgis drove across the U.S. in their Model A Ford roadster. They traveled 7,180 miles from New York to Los Angeles and back in forty-two days. They never stopped the car engine and drove the entire trip in reverse gear.

Travel Firsts

· **U.S. Admiral Richard Byrd** was the first person to fly over both the North and South Poles. In 1926, he flew from Norway over the North Pole and back in fifteen hours, thirty minutes. In 1929, he flew from Little America, Antarctica, over the South Pole and back in fourteen hours.

· **Captain Charles "Chuck" Yeager** was the first person to break the sound barrier. On October 14, 1947, in a U.S. Bell XS-1 rocket plane, he reached Mach 1.015 (670 miles per hour), the first supersonic speed.

· **Captain Ed Beach** led the first underwater journey around the world in the submarine U.S.S. *Triton.* Traveling nonstop for 60 days and twenty-one hours, this U.S. vessel traveled 26,723 nautical miles.

· **U.S. astronauts Neil Armstrong and Edwin "Buzz" Aldrin** were the first people to land on the moon. Their lunar module landed on the moon on July 20, 1969.

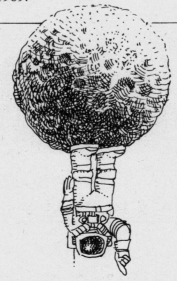

The Universe

Astronomy—the study of the universe—is one of the oldest sciences. Yet in the 1960s and early 1970s alone, astronomers made three of the most exciting discoveries ever: quasars, pulsars, and black holes. As one scientist put it, "The universe is not only queerer than we imagine, it is queerer than we *can* imagine."

Important Dates in the History of Astronomy

B.C.

c. 290 Aristarchus, a Greek scholar, proposed the theory that the earth revolves around the sun.

c. 240 Eratosthenes, a Greek scholar, measured the circumference and tilt of the earth and the size and distance of the earth in relation to the sun and moon.

240 The first recorded appearance of the comet later known as Halley's.

127 Hipparcus, a Greek astronomer, made the first known complete chart of the heavens, showing the positions of at least 850 stars.

A.D.

150 Ptolemy of Alexandria, a Greco-Egyptian, was the last great astronomer of ancient times. He showed the earth as a stationary globe in the center of the universe, with the sun, moon, and stars revolving around it in circular orbits at a regular rate.

1054 Chinese astronomers witnessed a supernova—the explosion of a dying star, when for an instant the star becomes a thousand times brighter.

1232 The first recorded use of rockets, by the Chinese against the Mongol invaders.

1543 Polish astronomer Nicholas Copernicus described the sun as the center of a great system, with the earth and all the planets revolving around it. This marked the birth of modern astronomy.

Heavenly Symbols

Sun ☉	Moon ☾	
Mercury ☿	Venus ♀	Earth ♁
Mars ♂	Jupiter ♃	Saturn ♄
Uranus ♅	Neptune ♆	Pluto ♇

The Heavenly Bodies Compared

Name	Mean distance from Sun (in millions km)	mi	Equatorial diameter (km)	(mi)	Density (water=1)	Circles Sun in	Turns on axis in
Sun	-		1,392,000	865,000	1.41	-	25.38d
Moon	-		3476	2160	3.34	-	27.32d
Mercury	58	36	4850	3015	5.40	88d	59d
Venus	108	67	12,140	7545	5.20	224.7d	244d
Earth	150	93	12,756	7926	5.52	365.25d	23:56h
Mars	228	142	6790	4220	3.95	687d	24:37h
Jupiter	778	484	142,600	88,600	1.34	11.9y	9:50h
Saturn	1427	887	120,200	74,700	0.70	29.5y	10:14h
Uranus	2870	1783	49,000	30,500	1.58	84.0y	10:49h
Neptune	4497	2794	50,200	31,200	2.30	164.8y	15:48h
Pluto	5900	3670	6400	3980	?	247.7y	153h

d=days; y=years; h=hours.

Facts About the Earth's Motions

• We cannot feel it, but the earth is moving. It spins once a day around its north-south axis. This is called rotation.

• The earth is also moving around the sun once a year. This is called revolution.

• The earth's axis of rotation now points very near the North Star, named Polaris. But the axis is spinning around so that it will tilt toward other stars in the future as it has in the past. The axis takes about 26,000 years to twist once around the sky.

• Because we are on the surface of the rotating sky, we are carried around to see different parts of the sky at different times of the day and during the year.

• At sunset, the sun doesn't really set. It stays in space and shines on different parts of the earth. Actually, when we see the sun "set," we are rotating into the shadow of the earth. *We* are setting into that shadow when we say the sun sets.

• At night, we see different parts of the sky as we are carried through different parts of the earth's shadow. So we see some stars "set" in the west as we lose sight of them. Other stars then come into view, rising in the east.

The Sun

• The sun is a star; like other stars in the universe, it is a globe of intensely hot, glowing gases.

• In the universe as a whole, the sun is not extraordinary; it's just an average star, neither very big nor very bright.

• The sun appears bigger and brighter than the other stars because it's only about 93 million miles from the earth. The next-closest star is some 25 million *million* miles away.

• To us on earth, the sun is vital, since it is practically the only natural provider of our energy and light.

• The sun pours out energy at all wavelengths of the electromagnetic spectrum, from gamma rays to radio waves.

• Only a fraction of the sun's total energy—about one two-thousandth million—falls on earth; but that fraction brings warmth, light, and life to what would otherwise be a cold, dark, dead lump of rock.

• We rely on the sun for food and fuel: Sunlight provides the energy for photosynthesis, by which plants make food; animals eat plants for food;

we live on animals and plants; fossil fuels such as coal, oil, and natural gas are the decayed remains of living organisms.

• Compared with the earth, the sun is gigantic. Although it is composed of gas, it still has 750 times as much matter as the rest of the solar system put together.

• The sun revolves around the Milky Way galaxy in 225 million years. It rotates on its own axis in the same direction as that of the planets (east to west) in about 25 days at its equator and 34 days at the poles.

SUN STATISTICS

Diameter, equator:	1,392,000 km, 865,000 mi	**Gravity:**	28 Earth's gravity
Volume:	1,303,600 Earth's volume	**Surface temperature:**	6000° C
Mean density:	1.41 (water=1)	**Core temperature:**	circa 15,000,000° C
Mass:	333,000 Earth's mass	**Spins on axis in:**	25-38 days
Mean distance from Earth:	149,000,000 km, 92,960,000 mi	**Orbits galaxy in:**	225 million years
		Velocity in orbit:	250 km/sec, 155 mi/sec

SUNSPOTS

• Sunspots are regions of strong magnetic fields that hold the sun's matter firmly in place.

• Sunspots are cooler areas seen on the surface of the sun. Being cooler, they do not shine as brightly as the surrounding area, so they appear dark.

• Sunspots range in size from very small to large enough to swallow the whole earth; so large, that they can be seen even without a telescope.

• Individual sunspots last from a few hours, for the small ones, to a few months, for the very large spots.

• At times, no spots are found on the sun. Sunspots appear gradually over the months until a large number of spots can be seen. Then their numbers get smaller, until there are none for days at a time.

• The time from minimum number of spots to minimum again is just over eleven years and is called the sunspot cycle.

SOLAR FLARES

• Solar flares are sudden, tremendous outbursts of energy on the sun. They most often occur in the neighborhood of sunspots.

• When a flare occurs, it sends out very strong X-rays and ultraviolet light. This energy is absorbed by our air, a few hundred miles above the earth, where it can affect shortwave radio waves.

• A strong flare sends out actual material in the form of electrically-charged atoms. A few days after the flare, these atoms crash into our atmosphere hundreds of miles above the earth's surface. The collisions make the air particles glow, which we see as northern lights, the aurora borealis.

• The great streams of solar gas seen sticking up prominently above the sun's surface in spectacular photos of the sun are not flares, but solar prominences. They seem to be controlled by strong solar magnetism.

The Moon

• The moon is the earth's natural satellite, circling our planet once every month.

• The moon is the earth's closest companion in space.

• Ancient peoples considered the moon a god or goddess and worshipped it; they also thought it influenced the mind, believing that too much exposure to moonlight, especially during the full moon, would drive a person mad. The word "lunatic" comes from *luna,* the Latin word for moon.

• The moon is a ball of rock with a diameter about a quarter that of the earth; it is much less dense than the earth, with a much smaller mass.

• The moon travels in an elliptical—elongated circular—orbit around the earth, always keeping the same side pointed toward us. Its closest point to the earth is called the perigee; its farthest point, the apogee.

• Because of its small mass, the force of gravity on the moon is only one-sixth that of the earth.

• The moon affects the earth's gravity, pulling the water in the oceans away from the earth, causing the twice-daily tides.

• Because of its small mass and low gravity, the moon cannot retain even a thin atmosphere; there is no sound on the moon, since sound waves need gas through which to travel. There is also very little light on this airless, waterless world.

• Without a blanketing atmosphere, there is a great contrast between day and night temperatures on the moon. Lunar noon is a boiling 212° F., while at lunar midnight, the temperature drops to -247° F.

• The shadows cast by lunar features are razorsharp because there is no air to scatter light into the shadows.

MOON FACTS

Diameter, equator:	3476 km, 2160 mi	Apogee:	406,700 km, 252,710 mi
Volume:	1/49 Earth's volume	Mean distance from Earth:	384,400 km, 238,860 mi
Mean density:	3.34 (water=1)	Spins on axis in:	27⅓ days
Mass:	1/81 Earth's mass	Orbits Earth in (sidereal month):	27⅓ days
Gravity:	1/6 Earth's gravity	Synodic month (new Moon-new Moon):	29½ days
Perigee:	356,400 km, 221,460 mi		

HARVEST MOON AND HUNTER'S MOON

As a rule, the moon rises nearly an hour later each day. But near the autumnal equinox in the Northern Hemisphere (September 23), the moon rises at about the same time, soon after sunset, for several days in succession. When the moon is full near that time, it shines brightly enough to allow farmers to complete their harvest. So this moon is called the harvest moon. In the Southern Hemisphere, the harvest moon is the full moon nearest the vernal, or spring, equinox (March 21). The full moon following the harvest moon is known as the hunter's moon.

Eclipses

• A solar eclipse occurs when the moon is between the earth and the sun, hiding the sun; the shadow of the moon falls on the earth.

• A lunar eclipse occurs when the earth is between the sun and the moon; the shadow of the earth falls on the moon.

• There are at least two eclipses of the sun within a 365-day period (yearly), averaging 346.62 days apart.

• There are sometimes no lunar eclipses in a year.

• The maximum number of eclipses in a year is seven; there might be two solar and five lunar, or three solar and four lunar.

The Constellations

• The six thousand or so stars that we can see in the night sky with the naked eye vary greatly in brightness. Many of the brighter stars make patterns in the sky, called constellations.

• Constellations are valuable in observational astronomy because they enable us to find a particular star quickly.

• The stars that make up a constellation are not usually grouped together in space; they just happen to be grouped together in the line of sight. In the constellation of Orion, the closest of the seven main stars is 303 light-years away, and the farthest is 1,825 light-years away.

• The ancient Babylonian, Egyptian, Chinese, Greek, and Arab civilizations were familiar with the constellations. The names by which we know the constellations today are Latin forms of the Greek names.

• The Greeks named some constellations for the gods, heroes, and heroines of their mythology, such as Hercules, Andromeda, and Cassiopeia. They named others for animals—Scorpio, the scorpion; Cygnus, the swan; and Leo, the lion. Others were named for everyday objects, such as Crater, the cup, and Libra, the scales.

• Some constellations do resemble what they are supposed to represent: Cygnus does look like a swan in flight, for example. But a lot of imagination is needed to see the resemblance in most of the constellations!

• Ptolemy, the last of the great ancient astronomers, listed 48 constellations; since then, another 40 have been added.

The Aurora Borealis And The Aurora Australis

• The aurora borealis, also called the northern lights, is a broad display of rather faint light in the northern skies at night.

• The aurora australis, which is similar, appears at the same time in the southern skies.

• The aurora appears in many different forms—sometimes as a quiet glow, almost foglike; sometimes as streamers; sometimes as a series of luminous expanding arcs.

• There are many colors, with white, yellow, and red predominating.

• The auroras are most vivid and most frequently seen at about 20 degrees from the magnetic poles, along the northern coast of the North American continent and the eastern part of the northern coast of Europe.

• While the cause of the auroras is not known for certain, there does seem to be a connection with sunspot and solar flare activity.

• The auroral displays appear at heights ranging from fifty to about six hundred miles and have given us a means of estimating the extent of the earth's atmosphere.

• The auroras are often accompanied by magnetic storms whose forces disrupt electrical communication.

Observatories

• There are more than two hundred major observatories, or astronomical research stations, located throughout the world.

• The Mount Palomar Observatory, near Pasadena, California, was built high in a dry, mountainous region, where conditions are best for observing the heavens. It houses the largest telescope in the United States, the 200-inch Hale telescope.

• The largest reflector in the Northern Hemisphere is the 236-inch mirror at the Special Astrophysical Observatory in the Caucasus region of the Soviet Union.

• The most powerful telescopes in the Southern Hemisphere include a 158-inch reflector at Cerro Tololo International Observatory in Chile, a 152-inch telescope at Siding Spring Observatory in Australia, and a 141-inch reflector at the European Southern Observatory in La Sille, Chile.

• The most prominent feature of a large modern observatory is the dome-shaped building housing the telescope.

• During the day, the dome is usually closed; then, as dusk falls, it opens to expose the telescope to the heavens.

• The dome revolves so that the telescope can make a 360-degree sweep of the sky.

Five Science Fiction Facts

1. Writer Isaac Asimov said there were three kinds of science fiction: "What if . . .;" "If only . . .;" and "If this goes on . . . ."

2. Science fiction was written as far back as the 2nd century B.C.! The Greek satirist Lucian wrote *True History,* a book of lies that made fun of adventure books. It described how a gigantic waterspout propelled a shipload of sailors from the Straits of Gilbralter to the moon, and what happened when they met the Moon King.

3. The 17th-century French writer Cyrano de Bergerac wrote books about imaginary trips to the moon and sun. How to get to the moon? "Attach bottles of dew to your body in the morning," he wrote, "and when the sun rises it will suck the dew, and your body, into space."

4. In 1865, the French novelist Jules Verne wrote the book *From the Earth to the Moon.* He put travelers inside a projectile and fired them to the moon from a nine-hundred-foot-long cannon. With a charge of four hundred thousand pounds of guncotton (an explosive product), the projectile would be boosted to a speed of some seven miles a second. Verne placed the launching site in Florida. It was later found that at such a speed, the projectile would have been vaporized by the heat of friction with the earth's atmosphere. But Verne was right about the speed the projectile needed: It is the earth's escape velocity (the speed that a moving object must have to escape the earth's gravitational field). And his launching site is a stone's throw from the launching pad of the first real manned flight to the moon in 1969!

5. H.G. Wells, the English journalist and author, wrote *War of the Worlds* in 1898. He described an invasion by Martian war machines, which devastated the countryside with flamethrowers and death rays. In the U.S., in 1938, actor-writer-director Orson Welles adapted *War of the Worlds* for American radio. Thousands of listeners, thinking it was a real news bulletin, fled their homes to escape the Martians.

Weather

"Everybody talks about the weather, but nobody does anything about it."* Now, you can read all about it in this chapter. Weather facts such as winds of the world, weather spectacles, animal weather forecasters, and the significance of clouds can all be found here.

How's the Weather?

WEATHER SPECTACLES

LIGHTNING
A discharge of electricity from one cloud to another or between a cloud and earth.

Forked lightning appears as a jagged streak.

Heat lightning, as a series of flashes.

Ball lightning, as a bright ball.

It is estimated that lightning strikes one hundred times per second at any given moment around the world.

RAINBOW

When sunlight passes through raindrops, the water bends the light rays and forms bands of color. The most brightly-colored rainbows occur when the raindrops are large. A rainbow can only be seen by a person when his or her back is to the sun.

RED SNOW

Snow colored red by airborne dust or by the growth of red-colored algae in the upper layer of snow.

ST. ELMO'S FIRE

A flaming spark seen in stormy weather on points of airplanes and ships. Usually bluish green, sometimes white, it is often accompanied by a crackling noise.

THUNDER

The sudden and tremendous heat from lightning causes shock waves in air that expands rapidly. Because light travels faster than sound, lightning is seen before thunder is heard.

Rolling thunder occurs from long flashes of lightning or from clouds and mountains that cause echoes. At any given moment throughout the world, two thousand thunderstorms are in progress.

INSTRUMENTS FOR MEASURING WEATHER

Anemometer—Measures wind speed and force.

Barometer—Measures air pressure.

Ceilometer—Measures cloud height.

Hygrometer—Measures humidity.

Pluviometer—Measures rainfall.

Psychrometer—Measures relative humidity (water vapor in the air at a given temperature).

Sunshine Duration Transmitter—Measures number of hours of direct sunlight in a day.

Thermometer—Measures air temperature.

WEATHER FORECASTS

Fair weather will often remain when:

- The wind blows from the west or northwest.
- The morning fog burns off by noon.
- Cumulus clouds dot the afternoon sky in the summer.

Rainy or snowy weather will often come when:

- The north wind shifts to the west and then to the south.
- The sky is dark to the west.
- There is a ring around the moon.

Air temperatures will often rise when:

- The wind is from the south with cloud cover at night.

Air temperatures will often fall when:

- The wind blows from the north or northwest.
- The sky is clear at night and the wind is light.

Fair weather will often come when:

- The wind shifts to the west.
- The clouds rise.

A GRAB BAG OF WEATHER FACTS

DOG DAYS
The dog days of summer occur in the Northern Hemisphere between early July and early August. They are days of hot, humid weather named after the dog star, Sirius, which rises in the sky at this time.

INDIAN SUMMER
This is the name given to mild, calm, hazy weather that occurs in late autumn. It may occur once or several times in the fall. The origin of the term Indian summer is not known. It may have been a reference to the warm weather of India.

SLEET AND HAILSTORMS
Sleet is rain that passes through cold air and freezes. Hailstorms are born high in thunderclouds. As hail is caught in updrafts and downdrafts, it becomes enlarged by coatings of ice.

SNOW
The rule of thumb is that it takes ten inches of snowfall to equal one inch of rain.

ANIMAL FORECASTERS

The predictions below are popular weather superstitions.

- If dogs eat grass, there will be rain, maybe a storm.
- If a pig carries straw in its mouth, a storm is on the way.
- If sheep feed on a hill, good weather is ahead.
- Gulls flying inland indicate severe gales (heavy winds).
- When cricket chirps grow long or strong, a storm is coming.

Winds

WINDS OF THE WORLD

The local winds of various countries and regions of the world have been given special names. Below is a partial list and description of some of these winds.

Berg Wind   A coastal wind in South Africa that is hot, dry, and blows offshore.

Bora   A cold, dry wind that blows along the coasts of Yugoslavia and Italy in the Adriatic Sea.

Buran   A bitterly cold wind in the U.S.S.R. that often carries snow and blizzard-like conditions.

Chinook   A warm, dry wind that blows from the eastern slopes of the Rocky Mountains in Canada and the U.S.

Föhn   A warm, dry wind that blows down the slopes of the European Alp mountains.

Khamsin   A hot, dry wind that blows from the Sahara Desert, affecting the countries of Egypt, Lebanon, Israel, and Syria.

Lereche	A hot, dry wind of southern Spain that blows from North Africa.
Mistral	A strong, cold wind that blows in southern France.
Monsoon	A seasonal wind in Asia, caused when wind direction reverses and blows off the Indian Ocean. This kind of wind is also known as a monsoon in East and West Africa and Australia.
Pampero	A strong, cold wind of South America that blows east from the Andes Mountains across the South American pampas (prairies).
Santa Ana	A strong, hot wind that blows from the north, northeast, or east in southern California.
Shamal	A hot, dry, persistent wind that blows in the summer in Iraq and the Persian Gulf.
Sirocco	A warm, southerly wind of the Mediterranean region, especially common in Italy, Sicily, and Malta. It blows from North Africa and is very humid when it reaches Italy and its nearby islands.
Sukhovey	A warm, dry wind of southern Russia.

A GRAB BAG OF WIND FACTS

CYCLONE
A severe tropical storm with intense circular winds often accompanied by heavy rains.

DOLDRUMS
This is an old term used by sailors to describe a belt of light winds in the tropical and equatorial latitudes. Today, meteorologists call this wind belt the ITCZ or Intertropical Convergence Zone.

HABOOBS
A sudden violent windstorm in the Sudan, Africa. These intense sandstorms usually last about one hour.

HURRICANE
In the Caribbean and the United States, the name for tropical cyclones. Hurricanes feature winds of over 74 m.p.h., rain, thunder, and lightning.

If the heat released by a hurricane in one day were converted to electricity, it could fulfill the electrical needs of the U.S. for more than six months.

The eye or center of a hurricane averages a width of fourteen miles. The winds in the eye are less than 15 m.p.h. compared to the 74 m.p.h. winds of the outer part of the hurricane.

MICROBURSTS
Also known as "wind shear," these are sudden high-altitude wind shifts that often plague aircraft during takeoffs and landings. Microbursts may blow up to 80 m.p.h. for a short period of time.

TORNADO
A violent, destructive, funnel-shaped whirlwind that travels in a narrow path over the land.

A two-hundred-mile-long area in the U.S. that stretches along the Oklahoma-Texas border is known as "Tornado Alley." The most active tornado weather in the world is located there.

The strongest winds of any natural storm are located at the base of tornadoes; these winds average up to 250 m.p.h.

Tornadoes are sometimes off-shoots of hurricanes that hit land.

TRADE WINDS
These are steady winds found over most oceans in the tropics. They blow toward the equator from the north in the Northern Hemisphere and toward the equator from the south in the Southern Hemisphere. In the days of shipping by sail, they were called the "winds that blow trade," then shortened to "trade winds."

TYPHOON
A violent tropical cyclone occurring in the region of the Philippines or the China Sea.

WILLY-WILLIES
In Australia, a term for violent tropical cyclones.

ZEPHYR
This gentle breeze from the west was named after the Greek god of the west wind, Zephyrus.

THE BEAUFORT WIND SCALE

British admiral, Sir Francis Beaufort (1774-1857), devised a scale to measure wind strength for the sailing ships of his time. The Beaufort Scale has been adapted and modified for use on land today.

Beaufort Number	Miles Per Hour	What It Is Called	Description
0	Less than 1	Calm	Smoke moves straight up
1	1-3	Slight Wind	Wind shown by smoke drift
2	4-7	Light Breeze	Face feels wind; leaves rustle
3	8-12	Gentle Breeze	Leaves move constantly
4	13-18	Moderate Breeze	Wind blows dust
5	19-24	Fresh Breeze	Small trees with leaves move
6	25-31	Strong Breeze	Large branches move
7	32-38	High Wind	Large trees sway; walking against wind is difficult
8	39-46	Gale	Small branches snap off trees
9	47-54	Strong Gale	Slight damage to buildings
10	55-63	Storm	Greater damage to buildings; trees uprooted
11	64-73	Violent Storm	Widespread damage
12	74-136	Hurricane	Extreme damage; devastation

Clouds

• **"Cloud nine"** is a term once used by the U.S. Weather Bureau to describe the highest and least threatening type of cloud. In everyday speech, a person who is very happy is sometimes said to be "on cloud nine."

• **Halos,** luminous circles, around the sun and moon are formed by light shining through cirrostratus clouds.

• **Noctilucents,** as the highest clouds are called today, are probably formed by meteor dust. They appear fifty miles high in the western sky after sunset. Noctilucents travel at a speed of 394 miles per hour.

• A **"mackerel sky"** is formed by the wavelike patterns of cirrocumulus clouds that look like the skin of mackerel fish.

• **"Mare's tails"** are the feathery strands in the sky made when cirrus clouds are blown about.

TEN MAJOR TYPES OF CLOUDS

Name	Description	What May Fall	Height
Cirrus	Thin, wispy clouds made of ice crystals	Nothing	4 miles or more
Cirrocumulus	Thin, patchy clouds made of ice crystals	Nothing	4 miles or more
Cirrostratus	Thin layers of gauze-like clouds made of ice crystals	Nothing	4 miles or more
Altocumulus	Patches or layers of white or gray puffy clouds	Drizzle or snow flurries	1 to 4 miles
Altostratus	Gray or blue layers of gauzy clouds made of ice crystals	Light rain or snow	1 to 4 miles
Stratocumulus	Gray clouds with dark shading in rolling or puffy layers	Drizzle or snow flurries	¼ to 1 mile
Stratus	Low sheets of gray clouds seen in the winter	Drizzle or snow flurries	0 to 1 mile
Nimbostratus	Dark, wet-looking clouds, often with streaks of rain extending to the ground	Steady rain or snow	0 to 1 mile
Cumulus	White puffy detached clouds of constantly changing shapes	Nothing	¼ to 4 miles
Cumulonimbus	Heavy dense clouds, also called "thunderheads"	Heavy rain, snow, or hail	¼ to 4 miles

The World

Explore the world you live in: the earth below, the sky above. Discover what makes the ocean salty, which country is called the Emerald Isle, and what is twilight. Explanations and definitions of planet Earth, our world, are found here.

The Earth

VITAL STATISTICS

• The earth is the third planet from the sun. It is the fifth largest of the nine planets of the solar system. The sun is one of approximately 120 billion stars in the Milky Way galaxy. The Milky Way is one of uncountable other galaxies in the universe.

• The earth is about 4.55 billion years old.

- It weighs 6.68 sextillion, 588 quintillion short tons.
- The earth's area is about 197 million square miles.
- The diameter of the equator is 7,926 miles.
- The polar diameter is 7,900 miles.
- The circumference around the poles is 24,860 miles.
- The **crust** is the outer layer of the earth. Made of rock, the crust is from five to 25 miles thick. The continents and ocean basins (bottoms) make up the earth's crust.
- The **mantle** extends 1,800 miles beneath the earth's crust. It is made up of molten rock which is 1,600° F in the upper area. The temperature of the mantle increases to over 4,000° F down where it meets the earth's core.
- The earth's **core** consists of the outer liquid core, which is 1,400 miles thick and is made of molten iron and nickel, and the solid inner core, a ball of iron and nickel with temperatures of over 7,200° F. It is solid because of the pressure extended upon it. The diameter of this ball is about 1,600 miles.
- Water covers 71 percent of the earth's surface; 29 percent of the earth's surface is land.

THE EARTH'S ATMOSPHERE

The atmosphere that surrounds the earth like an invisible skin is a mixture of protective gases, weighing some 5,000 million tons.

Layers of Atmosphere

Troposhere—The lowest layer, about 10 miles thick. It is here that weather systems are born.

Stratosphere—A calm layer that extends about 30 miles above the earth. Within it is the ozone layer (ozone is a form of oxygen).

Mesosphere—A cold layer about 50 miles above the earth.

Thermosphere—A layer, about 400 miles above the earth, which contains the ionosphere, a high concentration of charged particles that reflect radio waves.

Exosphere—The outer fringe of the atmosphere.

Bodies of Water

OCEANS

What They Are and Why They Are Salty

An ocean is a huge collection of water that separates the continents. Ocean water is salty because the rivers that flow into it carry salts from the land. Over millions of years, the oceans have become more and more salty because when ocean water evaporates, the salts remain in the ocean.

Pacific Ocean

Location: Between Asia and Australia in the west and North and South America in the east.

Size: About 64 million square miles.

Average Depth: 12,925 feet.

Deepest Point: The Mariana Trench, near the island of Guam; 35,840 feet deep.

• The Pacific is larger in area than all the land on the earth.

• The highest recorded wave was sighted in the Pacific in 1933. It was 112 feet high.

Atlantic Ocean

Location: Separates North and South America from Europe and Africa.

Size: About 32 million square miles.

Average Depth: 11,730 feet.

Deepest Point: Puerto Rico Trench, north of the West Indies; 28,232 feet deep.

• The Atlantic Ocean is widening an inch every year.

• The Atlantic is the most important ocean for commerce because the chief industrial countries of the world lie along its coastline.

Indian Ocean

Location: Between Africa, Asia, and Australia.

Size: About 28 million square miles.

Average Depth: 12,598 feet.

Deepest Point: The Java Trench, south of Indonesia; 23,376 feet deep.

• The Indian Ocean is the world's greatest source for offshore oil.

• The Indian Ocean floor, along with the Arctic Ocean floor, are the least explored regions in the world.

Arctic Ocean

Location: Centers around the North Pole.

Size: About 5 million square miles.

Average Depth: 3,407 feet.

Deepest Point: The Eurasia Basin; 17,881 feet deep.

• The Arctic is the smallest, shallowest, most northerly, and coldest of all the oceans. Much of the Arctic Ocean lies beneath ice.

OTHER BODIES OF WATER

Bay—An inlet of the sea. The largest is Hudson Bay in Canada.

Bayou—A sluggish, marshy creek. This term is used in the lower Mississippi River area.

Estuary—The water at a river's mouth where fresh and salt water are mixed.

Geyser—A hot spring of water that erupts intermittently. Geysers are found in Iceland, New Zealand, and North America (e.g., "Old Faithful" in Yellowstone National Park).

Glacier—Slow-moving mountains of ice. A glacier begins to move when its ice is 200 feet deep. Generally, glaciers move less than one foot a day.

Gulf—Part of the ocean or sea that extends into the land. A gulf is smaller than a bay. The largest is the Gulf of Mexico.

Iceberg—A mass of ice that floats in the ocean. About one-ninth of an iceberg's mass is visible above water. The largest known iceberg was 208 miles long and 60 miles wide. It was located in the Antarctic.

Lake—An inland body of standing water. Lake Superior in North America is the largest freshwater lake in the world. It is 31,700 square miles. Lake Baykal in the U.S.S.R. is the deepest lake in the world and has the most water of any freshwater lake. At its deepest point, it is 5,315 feet. It contains 5,520 cubic miles of water.

River—A natural stream of water. Most rivers flow into the oceans. Some flow into lakes or, in desert regions, simply trickle to an end. The world's longest river is the Nile in Africa. It is 4,160 miles long. The world's largest river is the Amazon in South America. It carries 157,000 cubic yards of water per second into the ocean.

Sea—A sea is an ocean that is sometimes partially or completely land-locked. Standard maps show approximately 77 seas around the world. The Sargasso Sea is noted for the calmness of its water amid the swirling ocean currents. Located in the North Atlantic between Florida and the Azores, it is awash with Sargasso seaweed and exotic sea life.

Waterfall—A steep descent of water caused by an abrupt change of the level of a river. The world's highest waterfall is Angel Falls in Venezuela, with a drop of 3,212 feet. The world's widest waterfall is the 2½-mile-wide Iguazu Falls in South America. It straddles the countries of Argentina and Brazil.

The Land

Highest Point: The highest point on earth is Mount Everest in Nepal and Tibet. It is 29,028 feet above sea level. (In 1987, new calculations, based on U.S. satellite measurements, indicated that the Himalayan peak K-2 may be a few feet higher than Mt. Everest.)

Lowest Point: The lowest point on earth is the Dead Sea in Israel and Jordan. It is 1,312 feet below sea level.

DESERTS

The World's Largest Deserts

- The Sahara in North Africa, 3.5 million square miles, the largest desert in the world
- The Arabian in the Near East, about one million square miles
- The Gobi in Asia, 500,000 square miles
- The Kalahari in Southern Africa, 225,000 square miles

Desert Facts

- Deserts are hot, arid lands that receive no more than 10 inches of rain a year.
- Only one-fifth of the Sahara Desert is covered with sand; the rest is covered with barren rock and sun-scorched rubble.
- The world's sandiest desert is the Arabian Desert.
- In the Sahara Desert, large areas of sand are called ergs.
- Except for Europe, all of the continents have deserts.

ISLANDS

The World's Largest Islands

- Greenland in the North Atlantic, 840,000 square miles
- New Guinea in the western Pacific, 306,000 square miles
- Borneo in the western Pacific, 286,100 square miles
- Madagascar in the Indian Ocean, 226,658 square miles
- Baffin in the Arctic Ocean, 195,928 square miles

Island Facts

- The largest island in the U.S. is Long Island, New York, which is 1,396 square miles.
- The world's newest island is a volcanic island in the Pacific Solomon Island chain. It began forming in 1979 and is still unnamed.

GRASSLANDS

Pampas—Areas of long grass in South America.

Plains—Areas of treeless, level land with short grass.

Prairies—Areas of long grass in North America.

Savannas—Moist tropical grasslands.

Steppes—Dry areas of treeless land with short grass in Southeastern Europe or Asian.

Veld—Grasslands of Southern Africa.

WETLANDS

Bog—A poorly-drained lake or pond that forms thick, wet vegetation with an "eye" of open water.

Marsh—An open area of wetland covered by water-loving grasses and cattails.

Quicksand—A pocket of ordinary sand saturated by water from an underground source that makes it soup-like.

Slough (sloo)—An American term for low-lying wetland.

Swamp—A wetland that is dominated by trees; a wet forest.

JUNGLES

• Jungles are tropical forests that are hot and steamy.

• The three regions of the world with jungles are Southeast Asia, western Africa, and central South America.

• Jungles are home for a great variety of wild animal life, poisonous plants, and bacteria that are threatening to man.

VALLEYS

Canyon—A deep valley with very high, steep slopes and sometimes a stream running through it.

Dale—Another word for valley.

Dell—A small, secluded valley usually covered with trees.

Dingle—A small, wooded valley.

Glen—A secluded narrow valley.

Gorge—A narrow, steep-walled canyon.

Gully—A deep trench worn in the earth by running water.

Hollow—A small valley.

Ravine—A deep, narrow valley with steep sides. It is larger than a gully and smaller than a canyon.

Vale—A poetic term for valley.

Valley—An elongated depression of earth, usually between mountains, hills, or high lands.

MOUNTAINS

Famous Mountain Peaks

Adam's Peak in Sri Lanka is a mountain considered to be sacred by three religious groups: Buddhists, Hindus, and Muslims.

Mauna Kea in Hawaii is the tallest mountain peak, measuring from its seabed to its peak. It is 33,476 feet high. Only 13,796 feet, or less than half of the mountain, is above ground.

Mt. Olympus, the highest mountain peak in Greece, was known as the "home of the gods" to the ancient Greeks.

Mt. Rushmore in the Black Hills of South Dakota is noted for its gigantic sculpture of four U.S. presidents. The heads of George Washington, Thomas Jefferson, Abraham Lincoln, and

Theodore Roosevelt have been carved in 70-foot-high likenesses. It took John Borglum and his son, Lincoln, fourteen years to carve the sculpture.

Mt. Ararat near the Turkish-Iranian border is, according to the Bible, the place where Noah's ark rested after the rains subsided.

Mt. Fuji in Japan is the most photographed and painted mountain in the world.

Mt. Huascaran in Peru was the first major peak climbed by a woman, Annie Peck, of Providence, Rhode Island, in 1908.

Mt. Sinai in Egypt is, according to the Bible, the mountaintop where Moses received the Ten Commandments.

Mt. Vesuvius in Italy erupted and engulfed the cities of Herculaneum, Stabiae, and Pompeii in A.D. 79.

Record-Book Mountains

Tallest mountain range: The Himalaya mountain range contains 96 of the world's 109 tallest peaks.

Tallest underwater mountain range: The Cordillera, which is in the Indian and East Pacific Oceans. Its average height is 8,000 feet above the base ocean depth.

Longest mountain range: The Andes in South America. They are 15,000 miles long.

Richest mountain range: The Andes are the most abundant mountain source of gold, silver, copper, and other valuable minerals.

Highest island mountain peak: Jaja Peak, West Irian, New Guinea, which is 16,503 feet above sea level or about 5 miles high.

Largest volcanic mountain: Mauna Loa in Hawaii is 13,680 feet high, with a crater 3 miles long and 1miles wide.

HIGH!

VOLCANOES

• The Ring of Fire is a belt of volcanoes that nearly encircles the Pacific Ocean. It includes more than half of the world's active volcanoes.

• Types of volcanic eruptions:

Hawaiian—Fluid lava that flows quietly from the crater.

Strombolian—Thick lava that flows in mild explosions.

Vulcanian—Violent explosions of lava as plugs blocking the volcano's vent are uncorked.

Pelean—Explosions that send an avalanche of incandescent gas and ash down the slopes of the mountain, destroying everything in its path.

Continents

NORTH AMERICA

• North America is the third largest continent.

• The world's largest group of freshwater lakes are located in North America: the Great Lakes.

• North America has the longest coastline of any continent. It is 96,000 miles long.

Population: 397.4 million (1985)

Size: 9,366,000 square miles

Highest point: Mt. McKinley, Alaska; 20,320 feet above sea level, almost 4 miles high

Lowest point: Death Valley, California; 282 feet below sea level

Largest country: Canada; 3,851,787 square miles

Most populous country: United States; 239.4 million (1986)

SOUTH AMERICA

- South America is the fourth largest continent.
- The world's longest mountain range, the Andes, are in South America. The Andes mountains are 15,000 miles long.
- Most of the people of South America live along the coastline of the continent.
- The southernmost city in the world, Punta Arenas, Chile, is located in South America.

Population: 263.3 million (1985)

Size: 6,881,000 square miles

Highest point: Mt. Aconcagua, Argentina; 22,834 feet above sea level, about 4⅓ miles high

Lowest point: Valdes Peninsula, Argentina; 131 feet below sea level

Largest country: Brazil; 3,286,470 square miles

Most populous country: Brazil; 135 million (1985)

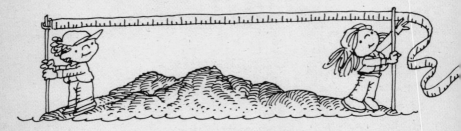

EUROPE

- Europe is the second smallest continent.
- The largest ice cave in the world is located in Europe. It is the Eisriesenwelt Cave in Austria.

Population: 673.9 million (1985)

Size: 3,997,929 square miles

Highest Point: Mt. El' Brus, U.S.S.R.; 18,510 feet above sea level, about 3½ miles high

Lowest point: Caspian Sea; 92 feet below sea level

Largest country: U.S.S.R.; 8,649,490 square miles

Most populous country: U.S.S.R.; 277.5 million (1985)

AFRICA

- It is the second largest continent.
- Africa is the warmest continent in the world.

  Population: 538 million (1985)

  Size: 11,688,000 square miles

  Highest point: Mt. Kibo, Kilimanjaro in Tanzania; 19,340 feet above sea level, about 3½ miles high

  Lowest point: Lake Assal, Djibouti; 510 feet below sea level

  Largest country: Sudan; 967,000 square miles

  Most populous country: Nigeria; 102.8 million (1985)

ASIA

- Asia is the world's largest continent. It covers one-third of the earth's land surface.
- More than one half of the people in the world live in Asia.
- Five of the longest rivers in the world are located in Asia. They are the Yangtse, Yensei, Yellow, Ob-Irtysh and Amur rivers.
- The highest point and the lowest point in the world are in Asia.

  Population: 3 billion (approximately, 1985)

  Size: 17,139,455 square miles

  Highest point: Mt. Everest, Nepal-Tibet; 29,028 feet above sea level, about 5½ miles high (new calculations indicate that the Himalayan peak K-2 may be a few feet higher than Mt. Everest)

  Lowest point: Dead Sea, Israel-Jordan; 1,292 feet below sea level, about 1½ miles below sea level

  Largest country: China, 3,769,000 square miles

  Most populous country: China; 1 billion (approximately, 1985)

AUSTRALIA

• This is the smallest continent
• It is the driest continent.
• Geologically, Australia is the oldest continent.
• It is the lowest continent in the world. One half of the continent (the Western Plateau) is only 1,000 feet above sea level.
• Australia is the only continent without active volcanoes.
• It is the only continent made up entirely of one country, which is Australia.

Population: 15.3 million (1985)

Size: 2,966,000 square miles

Highest point: Mt. Kosciusko; 7,310 feet above sea level, about 1⅓ miles high

Lowest point: Lake Eyre; 52 feet below sea level

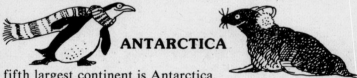

ANTARCTICA

• The fifth largest continent is Antarctica.
• Antarctica is the world's highest continent. It is covered by an ice sheet which averages a height of one mile above sea level.
• Antarctica is the coldest, emptiest, and most remote continent.
• The purest, driest air in the world surrounds this continent. There is no mold or mildew in Antarctica.
• During the winter, Antarctica is dark 24 hours a day.
• Nine-tenths of the ice in the world can be found in Antarctica.
• The Antarctic Treaty of 1962 guarantees that the continent will only be used for peaceful purposes such as research in biology, geology, and oceanography.

Population: Uninhabited

Size: 5.4 million square miles

Highest point: Vinson, Massif; 16,864 feet above sea level, about 3 miles high

Lowest point: Not known

Countries of the World

NAMES AND PLACES

Five Countries with Name Changes

- Tanzania was formed when Tanganyika united with Zanzibar.
- Thailand was once called Siam.
- Sri Lanka was once called Ceylon.
- Zaire was once called the Congo.
- Zimbabwe was once called Rhodesia.

Nicknames of Countries

- The Republic of Ireland is sometimes called the Emerald Isle.
- Tonga, in the Pacific Ocean, is known as the Friendly Islands.
- Australia is sometimes known as the "land down under."

World Cities and their Names

Amsterdam (Netherlands) means "dam on the Amstel River."

Athens (Greece) is named after Athena, the ancient Greek goddess of wisdom.

Belgrade (Yugoslavia) means "white city."

Brussels (Belgium) means "buildings on a marsh."

Buenos Aires (Argentina) means "good winds."

Chicago (U.S.) is from *checagore,* an American Indian word for a type of wild garlic that once grew in the area.

Copenhagen (Denmark) means "merchant's harbor."

Glasgow (Scotland) means "green hollow."

Madrid (Spain) means "timber."

Miami (U.S.) means "peninsula dwellers."

Munich (West Germany) means "monk." The city was built on the site of a monastery.

Quebec (Canada) means "place where the river narrows."

Shanghai (China) means "on the sea."

Names of Pacific Ocean Islands

Melanesia, Micronesia, and Polynesia are groups of islands in the Pacific Ocean.

• Melanesia means "black islands." It includes Fiji and the Solomon Islands.

• Micronesia means "little islands." It includes Wake and the Marshall Islands.

• Polynesia means "many islands." It includes Hawaii, the Line, Ellice, Phoenix, Tonga, Cook, and Samoa Islands, Easter Island, and French Polynesia.

WORLD GOVERNMENTS

Emirate—A country ruled by an emir (a native ruler of Asia or Africa); for example, Kuwait.

Monarchy—A country ruled by a king or queen because of heredity; for example, Saudi Arabia.

Principality—A country ruled by a prince; for example, Monaco.

Republic—A country governed by a president or similar leader and majority rule; for example, France and the U.S.

Sultanate—A country ruled by a sultan (king of a Muslim state); for example, Oman.

PEOPLES OF THE WORLD

Bantu—The word bantu means "people" and refers to the people of central, eastern, and southern Africa.

Kurds—These are agricultural and pastoral people who live in parts of Iran, Iraq, Turkey, Syria, and the U.S.S.R.

Maori—Polynesian peoples of New Zealand.

Moors—Muslims of Spanish or Turkish descent who speak Arabic and live in northwest Africa.

Mestizos—These are people who live in the countries of South America; they are of Indian and European origin.

Zulu—Bantu-speaking people who live in a reserved tribal area of the Republic of South Africa.

COUNTRIES AND THEIR LANGUAGES

- There are more than 250 languages spoken in Nigeria.
- The languages of Switzerland are French, Italian, and German.
- In Singapore, because of the mixed population, there are four official languages: Chinese, English, Malay, and Tamil.

THREE TINY COUNTRIES

1. **Liechtenstein** is a 62-square-mile country near Switzerland. The capital is Vaduz.
2. The **Maldive Islands** is a country southwest of India. It consists of 1,087 coral islands of which only 200 are inhabited. The country is 115 square miles, and the capital is Male.
3. **San Marino** is only 24 square miles. It is an ancient kingdom enclosed in the country of Italy. The capital of the country is also called San Marino.

CLUSTERS OF COUNTRIES

Eastern Europe is made up of eight Communist countries. They are Albania, Bulgaria, Czechoslovakia, East Germany, Hungary, Poland, Romania, and Yugoslavia.

Great Britain or the United Kingdom is made up of England, Northern Ireland, Scotland, and Wales.

The Low Countries are so called because they are located on flat land near sea level. The three countries in this group are Belgium, Luxembourg, and the Netherlands.

Time

THE INTERNATIONAL DATELINE

This is an imaginary line of longitude on the earth's surface located at 180°. It marks the place where travelers change dates. Those going east across the line subtract one day. Those going west across the line add one day. If not for this agreement, it would still be the same day for people traveling in an airplane westward around the earth for 24 hours, but it would be a day later for people on the ground.

TIME TERMS

Daybreak—The first light of day as the sun rises.

Dawn—The gradual increase of light as the sun rises.

Dusk—Semidarkness, as the light of the sun fades.

Midnight—The middle of the night: 12 o'clock A.M.

Noon—Midday: 12 o'clock P.M.

Twilight—The light of the sky at a time between full night and sunrise or between sunset and full night.

Fifty Questions Kids Ask

1. Who invented the baby carriage?
   ANSWER: Charles Burton, in 1848.
   SOURCE: *Famous First Facts,* 5th edition.

2. What and where is the tallest building in the world?
   ANSWER: The tallest office building is the Sears Tower on Wacker Drive in Chicago with 110 stories, rising to 1,454 feet.
   SOURCE: *Guinness Book of World Records,* 1986.

3. Who wrote the poem on the Statue of Liberty ("Give me your tired, your poor, your huddled masses yearning to breathe free")?
   ANSWER: American poet and essayist, Emma Lazarus. The poem's title is "The New Colossus."
   SOURCE: *Bartlett's Familiar Quotations,* 15th edition.

4. Which U.S. president had the most children?
   ANSWER: John Tyler had 15 children.
   SOURCE: *The World Almanac and Book of Facts, 1987.*

5. What does the term "turkey" mean in bowling?
   ANSWER: Three consecutives strikes.
   SOURCE: *Webster's New Collegiate Dictionary.*

6. What kind of farm did former President Richard Nixon's father own?
ANSWER: A lemon farm.
SOURCE: *McGraw-Hill Encyclopedia of World Biography.*

7. How long was the longest Monopoly game?
ANSWER: 660 hours.
SOURCE: *Guinness Book of World Records,* 1986.

8. Where did Charles Schulz, creator of the "Peanuts" comic strip, grow up?
ANSWER: Minneapolis, Minnesota.
SOURCE: *World Book Encyclopedia.*

9. Does Mother Goose have a son?
ANSWER: Yes, his name is Jack.
SOURCE: *Popular Nursery Rhymes: Mother Goose Rhymes with Explanations and Illustrations.*

10. How many chicken eggs would fit inside an ostrich egg?
ANSWER: 40.
SOURCE: *Macmillan Illustrated Animal Encyclopedia.*

11. What is Dorothy's last name in the *Oz* books?
ANSWER: Gale.
SOURCE: *Who's Who in Children's Literature.*

12. Where can I write for a pen pal?
ANSWER: International Friendship League, 22 Batterymarch St., Boston, MA 02109 or World Pen Pals, 1690 Como Avenue, St. Paul, MN 55108.
SOURCE: *Encyclopedia of Associations.*

13. Was there a real Indiana Jones, like the character in the film, *Raiders of the Lost Ark?*
ANSWER: The character was based loosely on archeologist and explorer Hiram Bingham (1875-1956).
SOURCE: *Hiram Bingham and the Dream of Gold,* by Daniel Cohen.

14. Why do earthworms come out on the sidewalks when it rains?
ANSWER: Because it breathes through its skin, an earthworm would drown if it stayed underground.
SOURCE: *World Book Encyclopedia,* under "Earthworms."

15. Why did President Abraham Lincoln grow a beard?
ANSWER: A twelve-year-old girl from New York wrote him a letter suggesting that a beard would improve his appearance.
SOURCE: *Lincoln: A Picture Story of His Life,* by S. Laurant.

16. In the Walt Disney movie *Pinocchio*, what was the cat's name?
ANSWER: Figaro.
SOURCE: *Animals' Who's Who,* by Ruthven Tremain.

17. What is the fastest land animal and how fast can it run?
ANSWER: The cheetah, which has been clocked at 71 miles per hour.
SOURCE: *Animal Superstars,* by Russell Freeman.

18. What are the names of the seven dwarfs in the Walt Disney movie *Snow White and The Seven Dwarfs?*
ANSWER: Bashful, Happy, Sneezy, Dopey, Grumpy, Doc, and Sleepy.
SOURCE: *Trivia Encyclopedia.*

19. What are the Seven Wonders of the Ancient World?
ANSWER: The Pyramids of Egypt; Hanging Gardens of Babylon; Statue of Zeus at Olympia; Temple of Artemis at Ephesus; Mausoleum at Halicarnassus; Colossus of Rhodes; The Pharos (Lighthouse) of Alexandria.
SOURCE: *World Book Encyclopedia.*

20. How do you make salt dough?
ANSWER: 1 cup flour, ½ cup salt, ½ cup water. Mix and knead dough for five minutes.
SOURCE: *Handprints: A Book of Recipes for Your Art Program.*

21. What is the world's fastest living creature?
ANSWER: On a power dive, a peregrine falcon can achieve a speed of 240 miles per hour.
SOURCE: *Animal Superstars,* by Russell Freeman.

22. How do you make a volcano model that really erupts?
ANSWER: Baking soda added to vinegar will produce the "volcanic" foaming.
SOURCE: *Science for All Seasons.*

23. The third world includes underdeveloped nations. What are the "first world" and "second world"?

    ANSWER: The first world is industrial nations; the second world is Communist European nations, as shown in a map produced by *Junior Scholastic* of the nations of the world.

24. What is a rhinoceros' horn made of?

    ANSWER: Karatin.

    SOURCE: *National Geographic Book of Mammals.*

25. Name four birds that "say" their names.

    ANSWER: Flicker, Bobwhite, Whipporwill, and Eastern Phoebe.

    SOURCE: *120 Questions and Answers About Birds.*

26. Where can I write to Michael J. Fox?

    ANSWER: c/o Lax Management, 9105 Carmelita Avenue #1, Beverly Hills, CA 90210.

    SOURCE: *The Address Book,* by Michael Levine.

27. Did the real-life Laura Ingalls Wilder have any brothers or sisters?

    ANSWER: She had three sisters, Mary, Carrie, and Grace.

    SOURCE: *20th Century Children's Writers.*

28. What are some endangered species?

    ANSWER: Chimpanzee, African elephant, and gorilla.

    SOURCE: *The World Almanac and Book of Facts, 1987.*

29. Who was the first woman in space?

    ANSWER: Valentina Tereshkova of the USSR was launched into space on June 16, 1963, in the spacecraft *Vostok 6.* Her trip lasted three days, during which time she made 49 orbits of earth.

    SOURCE: *The Doubleday Children's Almanac.*

30. What is the speed of light?

    ANSWER: In 1972, American scientist Kenneth M. Evenson found the speed of light to be 186,282.3959 miles per second. That means, in one second, light travels 186,282 miles, 697 yards.

    SOURCE: *How Did We Find Out About the Speed of Light?* by Isaac Asimov.

31. Which animal lives the longest?
ANSWER: The giant tortoise is known to live up to 177 years.
SOURCE: *The Doubleday Children's Almanac.*

32. When did dinosaurs live and how big were they?
ANSWER: The first dinosaurs appeared on earth more than 200 million years ago. They varied in size, but the most famous kinds included such giants as the apatosaurs, also called brontosaurs, which grew about 80 feet long.
SOURCE: *World Book Encyclopedia.*

33. Who was the Elephant Man?
ANSWER: John Merrick, a 19th-century Englishman, suffered from a severe form of neuroglibromatosis which so crippled and disfigured him that people labeled him the Elephant Man.
SOURCE: *The Elephant Man?* by Frederick Drimmer.

34. What makes the sound of thunder?
ANSWER: Lightning is a current of electricity that races from the ground to a cloud, or from one cloud to another. As it does so, it heats to a white-hot temperature of many thousands of degrees for a split second, and the air expands. When the lightning flash is over, the air cools and contracts again, coming together with a bang. That bang is the clap of thunder we hear.
SOURCE: *How did We Find out About the Speed of Light?* by Isaac Asimov.

35. What was the heaviest coin?
ANSWER: The 10-dalec piece, a coin which was minted in Sweden in the mid-seventeenth century. Each 44-lb. slab could purchase two cows.
SOURCE: *The Doubleday Children's Almanac.*

36. When did the first Jews come to America?
ANSWER: On September 1, 1654, a ship called the *Saint Charles* sailed into New Amsterdam Harbor (now New York Harbor) with twenty-three Jewish passengers fleeing from the Portuguese in Brazil. They established the first permanent community of Jews in what is now the United States.
SOURCE: *The Jews in America,* by Milton Meltzer.

37. How fast do bees fly?
ANSWER: Bees fly about 12 miles (19 kilometers) per hour.
SOURCE: *World Book Encyclopedia.*

38. When was the bicycle invented?

ANSWER: The first bicycle was built in the late 1700s by a Frenchman named DeSivrac. But the title "father of the bicycle" is usually given to a German, Baron Karl von Drais, who invented a two-wheeled bike around 1816.

SOURCE: *Compton's Encyclopedia and Fact Index.*

39. Is there really a Dr. Seuss?

ANSWER: Yes, but he is not a doctor. His real name is Theodore Seuss Geisel, and he was born in Springfield, Massachusetts, on March 2, 1904. His first book for kids was *And to Think That I Saw It on Mulberry Street,* which he wrote in 1937.

SOURCE: *Something About the Author.*

40. When did Disneyland open?

ANSWER: The original Disneyland in Anaheim, California, opened on July 17, 1955.

SOURCE: *Chase's Annual Events,* 1986.

41. How big was the biggest train?

ANSWER: The longest and heaviest train on record was one about 4 miles in length consisting of 500 coal cars. It weighed 47,250 tons.

SOURCE: *Guinness Book of World Records,* 1986.

42. Why do mosquito bites itch?

ANSWER: When a mosquito "bites," it stabs through the victim's skin with six needlelike parts called stylets, extracts the victim's blood, and fills the wound with its saliva. Most people are allergic to the saliva and an itchy welt called a "mosquito bite" forms on the skin.

SOURCE: *The World Book Encyclopedia.*

43. Why do stars twinkle?

ANSWER: When the light from stars reaches our atmosphere, it gets bent several times by layers of moving air.

SOURCE: *Childcraft—The How and Why Library.*

44. When was the first rodeo held?

ANSWER: In 1882, in North Platte, Nebraska.

SOURCE: *U.S. Trivia Trip Game Book,* 1986.

45. Who invented the computer? When was the first computer invented?

ANSWER: Vannevar Bush invented the analog computer in 1930. Howard Aiken invented the digital computer in 1944.

SOURCE: *Reader's Digest Almanac and Yearbook.*

46. Will the sun ever stop shining?
ANSWER: Yes, but not for billions and billions of years.
SOURCE: *Childcraft—The How and Why Library.*

47. What was the biggest fish ever caught?
ANSWER: Alfred Dean caught a 2,664-pound white shark off Ceduna, Australia on April 21, 1959.
SOURCE: The International Game Fish Association, 1986.

48. Could people live on Mars?
ANSWER: No. Temperatures on Mars range from -109°F to -24°F., and there is only a trace of oxygen in the planet's atmosphere. There is almost no liquid water.
SOURCE: *World Book Encyclopedia.*

49. How fast has the mile been run?
ANSWER: 3:46.32, by Steve Cram of Britain, in 1985.
SOURCE: *The World Almanac and Book of Facts, 1987.*

50. How many U.S. presidents have been assassinated?
ANSWER: Four. Abraham Lincoln, 1865; James A. Garfield, 1881; William McKinley, 1901; John F. Kennedy, 1963.
SOURCE: *The World Almanac and Book of Facts, 1987.*

What Do You Think?

THE KIDS' WORLD ALMANAC QUESTIONNAIRE

More than 3,000 students in the 5th grade were asked to answer twelve questions covering a broad range of topics in order to discover just what is on the minds of America's young people. The questionnaires were distributed throughout the United States, in both urban and rural areas, in order to obtain an accurate accounting of everyone's views.

Among the most interesting results from the poll was that 75 percent of those who responded named their family as the single most important part of their lives. In line with this strong feeling for one's family, the largest vote-getter when asked about the happiest moment of the past year was "taking a trip."

The results show that over 50 percent of the 5th graders believe that drug abuse is the number one problem in the world today. The second most serious problem according to the survey are the dangers of nuclear war.

The quality most admired in a friend was "kindness" according to more than 58 percent of the students. In this category, "loyalty" received 29 percent of the votes, whereas "popularity" and "appearance" received a combined total of only 5 percent.

On a less serious but equally vital topic, 45 percent of those polled said that *pizza* was the one food they couldn't live without. Ice cream finished a distant second in this category, and steak received the most votes among the write-in "others."

The complete survey and results are reprinted here in order to help you see where you "fit in" with your peers and where you maintain your individuality.

Many thanks to all of you (and your teachers) for your participation.

The Kids' World Almanac Questionnaire Results

(PERCENTAGE OF TOTAL FOLLOWS EACH ANSWER)

1. What do you think is the number one problem in the world today?
  a. pollution (5%)
  b. hunger (12%)
  c. terrorism (12%)
  d. drug abuse (55%)
  e. racism (1%)
  f. dangers of nuclear war (15%)

2. What quality do you most admire in a friend?
  a. loyalty (29%)
  b. kindness (58%)
  c. intelligence (7%)
  d. popularity (2%)
  e. appearance (3%)

3. How many kids, do you think, make up an ideal size family?
  a. one (4%)
  b. two (37%)
  c. three (26%)
  d. four (20%)
  e. more than four (13%)

4. What do you quarrel with your parents about most?
  a. school grades (12%)
  b. brothers and sisters (30%)
  c. spending money (11%)
  d. chores (23%)
  e. spare time activities (watching TV, listening to music, spending time with friends) (23%)

5. Which food do you think you couldn't live without?
  a. pizza (45%)
  b. hamburger (6%)
  c. ice cream (14%)
  d. French fries (7%)
  e. hot dog (2%)
  f. popcorn (6%)
  g. other (20%) (steak was the leader among "others")

6. What continent would you most like to visit?
   a. Africa (9%)
   b. Antarctica (6%)
   c. Asia (6%)
   d. Australia (25%)
   e. Europe (40%)
   f. South America (14%)

7. What job would you most like to have when you grow up?
   a. athlete (21%)
   b. astronaut (9%)
   c. lawyer (10%)
   d. news reporter (2%)
   e. doctor (10%)
   f. teacher (18%)
   g. other (30%) (veterinarian was the leader among "others")

8. At what age should a teenager "go steady"?
   a. 13 (26%)
   b. 14 (13%)
   c. 15 (19%)
   d. 16 (22%)
   e. 17 or over (20%)

9. If you could have been a member of a presidential family, which one would you have chosen?
   a. President Ronald Reagan's (40%)
   b. President George Washington's (18%)
   c. President Abraham Lincoln's (15%)
   d. President Theodore Roosevelt's (10%)
   e. President John Kennedy's (17%)

10. Which of the following is most important to you?
   a. family (75%)
   b. friends (7%)
   c. pet(s) (5%)
   d. school (4%)
   e. religion (9%)

11. Which of the following activities do you most like to do in your spare time?
   a. read (12%)
   b. watch television (20%)
   c. talk on the phone (14%)
   d. play a sport (30%)
   e. talk to your family or friends (6%)
   f. write letters (2%)
   g. listen to music (16%)

12. Which of the following was the happiest moment of this past year for you?
   a. getting a good grade on a test (18%)
   b. getting a new brother or sister (6%)
   c. meeting a new friend (18%)
   d. taking a trip (25%)
   e. winning a competition (15%)
   f. other (17%) (missing school was the leader among "others")

Index